The Effects of the California Voucher Initiative on Public Expenditures for Education

Michael A. Shires • Cathy S. Krop
C. Peter Rydell • Stephen J. Carroll

RAND

Institute on Education and Training

Supported by the
Lilly Endowment Inc.

RAND's Institute on Education and Training conducts policy analysis to help improve education and training for all Americans.

The Institute examines *all* forms of education and training that people may get during their lives. These include formal schooling from preschool through college; employer-provided training (civilian and military); postgraduate education; proprietary trade schools; and the informal learning that occurs in families, in communities, and with exposure to the media. Reexamining the field's most basic premises, the Institute goes beyond the narrow concerns of each component to view the education and training enterprise as a whole. It pays special attention to how the parts of the enterprise affect one another and how they are shaped by the larger environment. The Institute

- Examines the performance of the education and training system
- Analyzes problems and issues raised by economic, demographic, and national security trends
- Evaluates the impact of policies on broad, system-wide concerns
- Helps decisionmakers formulate and implement effective solutions.

To ensure that its research affects policy and practice, the Institute conducts outreach and disseminates findings to policymakers, educators, researchers, and the public. It also trains policy analysts in the field of education.

RAND is a private, nonprofit institution, incorporated in 1948, which engages in nonpartisan research and analysis on problems of national security and the public welfare. The Institute builds on RAND's long tradition—interdisciplinary, empirical research held to the highest standards of quality, objectivity, and independence.

This report summarizes the probable effects of California's upcoming school-voucher initiative on public spending for K–12 education in the state. These findings are based on a complex simulation analysis of enrollment, tax revenues, and other trends over the next decade.

Much of the debate over this initiative focuses on how vouchers might affect the quality of education. Although this issue is crucial, the initiative's fiscal effects are also important, for two reasons:

- Changes in spending may affect the quality of education.

- Spending on education has a strong effect on the state's budget.

Voucher advocates argue that only such a plan can avert California's looming fiscal crisis; opponents contend that by cutting funds for the public school system, vouchers may destroy this vital institution.

We do not take a position in this debate. Rather, we attempt to provide an analytic framework for evaluating such claims. Specifically, we examine the likely effects of Proposition 174 on:

- Total state spending for K–12 education.

- Spending per pupil in the public schools.

The research reported here was supported by a grant from the Lilly Endowment Inc. to RAND's Institute on Education and Training.

The work is intended to inform voters (who will[1] decide the issue in November), legislative and executive branch policymakers (who will be involved in implementing the initiative should it be approved), and policymakers in other states (who may seek to understand the fiscal implications of vouchers).

---

[1]This report was prepared before the November 2, 1993, election. Proposition 174 was, in fact, rejected by the California voters.

CONTENTS

FIGURES

On November 2, 1993, Californians will[1] vote on Proposition 174—the Parental Choice in Education Initiative. The proposition would establish a system of annual vouchers, funded by public tax dollars, that elementary and secondary students could use to pay tuition at private schools. The legislature would determine the value of the voucher, but it would equal at least one-half the prior year's total state spending per public school K–12 pupil, i.e., roughly $2,600.

Although much of the current public debate over Proposition 174 focuses on how it might affect the quality of education, its potential fiscal effects are also critical. Changes in spending can influence the quality of education, and total spending on education is a major component of California's overall budget.

To help illuminate these issues, we developed a simulation model of California school finance, along with forecasts of California's K–12 population and funding sources through academic year 2002–03. Using the model and forecasts, we attempted to predict the fiscal impact of Proposition 174. In particular, we addressed the following questions:

- Would public schools have more or less money per pupil?

- Would the state's overall cost for K–12 education be higher or lower?

---

[1]This report was prepared before the November 2, 1993, election. Proposition 174 was, in fact, rejected by the California voters.

The fundamental answer to both questions is simple: No one knows. In one sense, this is true in any debate on the fiscal effects of public policy; there is always some uncertainty. But the uncertainty in this case is of a completely different order. In the typical debate, analysts may argue about whether a new policy will cause a small fiscal effect or a large one, or perhaps whether it will have any fiscal effect at all. But in the case of vouchers, empirical analysis cannot tell us whether the fiscal effect will be strongly positive or strongly negative. Analysts cannot reliably predict whether vouchers will save money for California or will exacerbate the state's fiscal crisis. Similarly, it is not possible to predict whether spending per pupil in the public schools will go down or up. There are plausible arguments on both sides, but little definitive evidence.

In fiscal terms, then, Proposition 174 poses large risks, no matter how the electorate votes. Voting *for* the proposition may help avoid a fiscal crisis. But if relatively few students shift to private schools, or if certain provisions of the initiative are interpreted in certain ways, the proposition could actually worsen California's fiscal situation and, at the same time, could reduce the resources available to each public school pupil. Voting *against* Proposition 174, however, may court the serious risk that there is no better option for heading off the state's looming fiscal crisis.

THE BASELINE: CALIFORNIA'S IMPENDING FISCAL CRISIS

California will face a fiscal crisis over the next decade. In 1992–93, the state devoted 32 percent of its general fund revenues to K–12 education. If current trends continue, that fraction will rise to 43 percent by 2002–03. Since a large portion of California's general fund is consumed by nondiscretionary expenses, the projected increase in K–12 spending can come only at the expense of other discretionary programs, such as corrections and higher education. Yet most of these programs have already suffered significant budget reductions. *Without some change in school finance, it is difficult to see where the state will find the resources to meet the growing demands for K–12 spending.*

UNKNOWN DECISIONS, UNKNOWN EFFECTS

Advocates of Proposition 174 argue that the voucher system can help avert this fiscal crisis by reducing state spending on K–12 education. Opponents claim that spending will actually increase. This disagreement results, in part, from three fundamental unknowns:

1. How many students will shift from public to private schools?
2. What spending policy will the state pursue if vouchers are implemented?
3. How will certain provisions of Proposition 174 (the possible "double hit") be implemented?

We have reviewed the experiences of other voucher programs and have found none that can reliably answer these questions. Therefore, we have used our model to assess the likely fiscal outcomes of Proposition 174 for a variety of scenarios and alternatives. *In general, we find that the fiscal effects of Proposition 174 are highly uncertain. If it passes, California's total spending on K–12 education could rise— or fall. Likewise, total per-pupil public school spending could rise—or fall.*

IF FEW USE VOUCHERS, COSTS RISE

In general, the more students who leave the public system, the better the fiscal effects on the state budget. But we have found no reliable evidence that would help us predict how many students would use vouchers. Proponents assert that if Proposition 174 passes, 34 percent of the state's future public K–12 students will eventually turn to the private sector. At the other end of the spectrum, a study of private schools found that those schools would not expand dramatically under vouchers, thus effectively limiting the number of public school students who can shift. That study estimates that around 4 percent of the state's prospective public school K–12 population would shift to private schools. (Even such a small shift would require nearly a doubling of private school capacity.) We use these estimates to bound our analysis.

In Figure S.1 we present our prediction of the proposition's *average* fiscal impact over the next ten years, assuming the low-shift (4

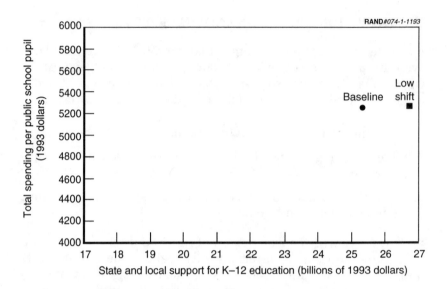

Figure S.1—If Few Students Shift, Total Cost Would Increase Without Increasing Per-Pupil Spending

percent) scenario. The point marked "Baseline" indicates what the state will be required to spend, on average, over the next decade if the voucher initiative does not pass: The average annual cost to the state would be $25.4 billion current dollars, with an average of $5,242 per pupil available to public schools.

The point labeled "Low Shift" indicates the fiscal effect of the voucher initiative if only 4 percent of California's public school students leave the public system. Per-pupil spending in the public schools would remain the same as without vouchers, but the state's cost would increase by an average of $1.2 billion a year. *Thus, if few students use vouchers, the state would spend more on K–12 education, but not on public school pupils.*

IF MANY USE VOUCHERS, COSTS FALL

If many students leave the public system, the fiscal effects of Proposition 174 would be much more positive. Figure S.2 shows the effects of a high-shift scenario (along with the baseline and low-shift

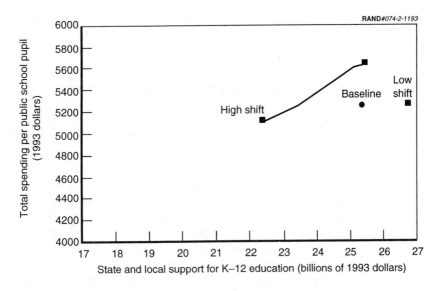

Figure S.2—If Many Students Shift, Fiscal Options Would Improve

results already discussed), again averaged over a ten-year period. The line labeled "High Shift" represents the variety of policy choices the state would have if 34 percent of the public school students left the public sector. The lower endpoint represents the minimum that the state would have to spend on K–12 education (as mandated by Propositions 98 and 111) and the associated level of resources available to public schools. The higher endpoint represents the maximum level of spending for the range of state spending policies we evaluated in this study. The line between the two points represents the range of options available to the state: from an average saving of $3.1 billion a year (if state policymakers choose to spend the minimum required on K–12 education, thus reducing per-pupil spending by 3 percent) to spending the same total amount on K–12 education (thus increasing the total resources available to public school pupils by about 7 percent per pupil).

If many students use vouchers, all the options are fiscally preferable to the current baseline. Many tradeoffs are available between reducing state spending and increasing per-pupil resources—some presumably better than others—but the entire set of choices is clearly attractive. *Unfortunately, there is no way to predict whether those choices will in fact be available,* or whether the low-shift scenario (with its higher total cost but no gain in per-pupil spending) would result.

THE "DOUBLE HIT" INCREASES UNCERTAINTY

This uncertainty is compounded by the interpretation of how vouchers and scholarship-redeeming students will be accounted for under Proposition 98. Voucher opponents allege that under certain circumstances, public school students changing to private schools would cause public schools to lose twice (the "double hit")—first by their removal from the base used to calculate the schools' guaranteed minimum budget and then again by the cost of their scholarships and the savings realized by the public schools being counted in that budget. Proponents respond that the authors of Proposition 174 clearly did not intend this outcome and that an "appropriate" implementation would not produce this effect. This dispute would have to be resolved by the legislature and possibly the courts. The final decision will have a profound effect on California school finance under Proposition 174.

Figure S.3 shows the fiscal effect of Proposition 174 for a range of legislative options for both high-shift and low-shift scenarios if a double hit does occur. If there is a large shift of students, the level of support to public schools could fall by as much as 18 percent, yielding a savings to the state of 29 percent. (Or per-pupil spending could be increased with no increase in total state costs.) On the other hand, if only a few students shift to private schools, state spending per public pupil could fall by 11 percent, while total state spending would drop by only 10 percent. (Or per-pupil spending could be held at current levels, but only by increasing total spending by 4 percent.) *If the"double hit" does take place, even more options are open. Again, the range of choices may be more attractive than the baseline or less attractive.*

THE BOTTOM LINE: CHOOSING AMONG RISKS

The decision on the double-hit issue will have a tremendous influence on the effects of the voucher initiative on state K–12 finance.

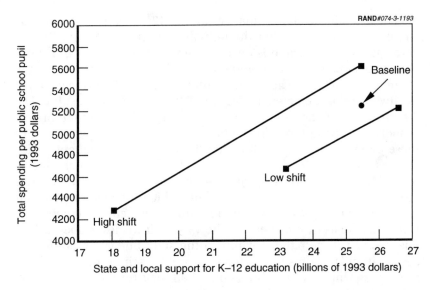

Figure S.3—The "Double Hit" Would Create More Choices

But *with or without the double hit, the fiscal effects of Proposition 174 are clearly quite uncertain. They may be positive or they may be bleak.* A shift of many students from public to private schools could present the state with choices among positive outcomes. In that situation, the choice for state policymakers would generally be between increasing the resources to the public schools (on a per-student basis), reducing overall spending on K–12 education (and mitigating the state's financial crisis), or some of both. On the other hand, if few students shift, the state will be faced with the less pleasant choices of reducing overall resources at public schools, increasing public spending on K–12 education, or both—difficult choices in light of the crisis presented above. Unfortunately, there are no definitive data to indicate which of these scenarios is more likely.

HOW THE FISCAL EFFECTS OF THE INITIATIVE WILL UNFOLD

In assessing these results, it is helpful to compare Proposition 174 to a game: Four players, in turn, will determine the initiative's fiscal effects on both the state's finances and K–12 education. The *voters* will play, deciding whether the initiative will happen at all. If they vote against it, the game is over. If they vote for it, the *courts* will have to decide the interpretation of the initiative with respect to the "double-hit" debate. The results of that decision will decide which of the two worlds depicted in Figures S.2 and S.3 will result. The *parents* will play their turn by either shifting their children to private schools or leaving them in public schools. The aggregate level of these parents' decisions will define the range of subsequent policy choices available to the state; parents will decide which line is operational in each of the figures—the high-shift line, which offers attractive choices, or the low-shift line, which forces more difficult tradeoffs than California would face without vouchers. Finally, the *state* will take its turn by deciding how much it wishes to spend. The final result will be either savings to the state budget or additional costs; either more resources for each public school pupil or fewer resources. Until *all* four players have had their turn, there is no way of knowing.

In sum, these findings represent a word of caution to both sides of the voucher debate. To those who believe that Proposition 174 is a good idea: The effects of the initiative could damage both state and public school finances. To those who believe that the voucher initiative is a bad idea: A crisis is approaching in California's public finance system, and the voucher initiative could help avoid even greater risks to come.

ACKNOWLEDGMENTS

Many people have contributed to this effort; we thank them all. We have received assistance and advice from staff members of several state agencies, including the Commission on State Finance, the Department of Education, the Department of Finance, and the Office of the Legislative Analyst. In addition, we are also indebted to Larry Picus at USC for helping us understand the intricacies of Propositions 98 and 111, and to Michael Heise at the Hudson Institute for helping us understand the Indianapolis voucher experiment.

Several RAND colleagues, including Randy Ross, David Feingold, Dick Buddin, and Bob Schoeni, contributed to the development and implementation of this analysis. Mitchell Wade was invaluable in the final preparation of this report.

We are also grateful to Carol Bingham and Bob Loessberg-Zahl at the Office of the Legislative Analyst, David Barulich at the Excellence through Choice in Education League (ExCEL), and Ned Hopkins at the California Teachers Association for their insightful comments on an earlier draft.

While we recognize the contributions of the many people who made this report possible, we emphasize that the discussion and findings in this report reflect only the views of the authors.

Chapter One

INTRODUCTION

On November 2, 1993, California voters will vote on Proposition 174—the Parental Choice in Education Initiative.[1] The proposition would establish a system of annual scholarships (vouchers), paid by the state with public tax dollars, to resident elementary and secondary students. The vouchers could be used to partially, or fully, defray tuition at public and private "scholarship-redeeming schools." The legislature would determine the value of the voucher, but it must equal at least one-half the prior year's total spending per public K–12 pupil.

Much of the debate over Proposition 174 is familiar: The likely effect of a voucher plan on the quality of education has been the topic of analysis and discussion in the United States for three decades.[2] While the empirical evidence is scanty, the issues are clear and the arguments well understood.

However, one aspect of the debate over Proposition 174 raises a new set of issues: the likely effects of the proposition on state spending for K–12 education. Proposition 174's advocates argue that it is

---

[1]This report was prepared before the November 2, 1993, election. Proposition 174 was, in fact, rejected by the California voters.

[2]Although there were experiments with voucher-type programs in England and Wales in the late 1800s, U.S. interest in vouchers dates from Milton Friedman, *Capitalism and Freedom*, The University of Chicago Press (Chicago, 1962). Brendan A. Rapple, "A Victorian Experiment in Economic Efficiency in Education," *Economics of Education Review*, Vol. 11, No. 10, December 1992, pp. 301–316, describes the early experiments.

needed to avert a looming fiscal crisis;[3] its opponents argue that its implications for public school spending threaten to destroy a critical social institution—the public school system.[4] Because both voucher advocates and opponents have traditionally focused on the quality issues, prior analyses of voucher plans have paid little attention to their implications for state spending for education.[5] There is no analytic framework for evaluating these claims.

This report presents the results of an analysis of the effects of Proposition 174 on public spending for K–12 education. Specifically, we examine the impacts of Proposition 174 on the resources available to public K–12 institutions (in total and per student) and the cost to the state of providing K–12 education to its residents.

We do not suggest that Proposition 174's effects on state spending for K–12 education should be determinative, or even that they are as important as its effects on the quality of education. But we do argue that these effects are important, both because education spending can affect education quality and because education spending has dramatic effects on California's entire state budget. Thus, fiscal effects need to be considered in evaluating the proposition.

PROPOSITION 174

About $5,200 will be spent, on average, on each California public school pupil in the 1993–94 school year. If the initiative passes, the value of a voucher next year would be at least half that amount, or $2,600.

Any K–12 student in California would be eligible for a voucher should he or she attend a "scholarship-redeeming school." Scholarship-redeeming schools are required to comply with the guidelines for pri-

---

[3]See, for example, Benjamin Zycher, "A Parental Primer on Vouchers," *The Los Angeles Times,* September 7, 1993, p. B5.

[4]See, for example, Ramona Ripston, "A Measure Built on a Foundation of Lies," *The Los Angeles Times*, September 7, 1993, p. B5.

[5]For example, the December 1992 issue of the *Economics of Education Review* was devoted to: "Market Approaches to Education: Vouchers and School Choice." The effects of voucher plans on state spending for education was not even mentioned in any of the articles.

vate schools in effect October 1, 1991; it is generally agreed that these guidelines present no unreasonable barriers to new or existing private schools. Scholarship-redeeming schools may not discriminate on the basis of race, ethnicity, or national origin; and they may not advocate unlawful behavior. But they are allowed to refuse admission to children on other grounds such as gender, disabilities, religious beliefs, behavior, or need for special services.

The initiative also specifies a minimum school size (25 students) and prohibits the imposition of "unnecessary, burdensome, or onerous regulation"[6] on scholarship-redeeming schools.

Proposition 174 also includes language designed to modify the calculations prescribed in Propositions 98 and 111, enacted in 1988 and 1990, respectively. These calculations establish a minimum state budget for K–12 education, depending on the state's General Fund revenues, property tax revenues, and enrollments in K–12 public schools.

Finally, the initiative contains guidelines for converting public schools into scholarship-redeeming schools and for the transition of staff and teachers between the two categories of schools. The initiative also contains a timeline for implementation.

THE "EDUCATIONAL QUALITY" DEBATE

The debate over education vouchers has traditionally focused on their likely effects on the quality of education. Advocates argue that vouchers would bring marketplace incentives to the schools. Faced with competition for students, teachers and administrators will have to become more efficient, innovative, and responsive to students' needs. Opponents generally respond that vouchers would result in an inequitable, discriminatory educational system: Private schools would search out and accept only able, well-behaved, easily taught students, leaving "less attractive" students—for example, the mentally, physically, or emotionally disabled—concentrated in a residual public school system. Profiteers would take advantage of the unsophisticated, and organizations advocating religious, racist, or

---

[6]Proposition 174, proposed Constitution Section 17, subdivision (b), paragraph (4).

ideological perspectives would receive support from the public sector.

While the issues are straightforward, few empirical data are available because of the very limited implementation of voucher programs both in the United States and in comparable industrialized countries.

Several school districts across the country have explored school choice programs in which different schools adopted various specialized curricula (e.g., emphasizing the performing arts or the physical sciences) or educational approaches (e.g., an emphasis on individualized instruction), and students were allowed to choose which school they would attend. In the early 1970s, for example, the Alum Rock School District in San Jose, California, tested a choice system by establishing several mini-schools at each public school and allowing parents the choice of enrolling their children in mini-schools in their own area or at a neighboring site. Similarly, in the late 1980s, Richmond, California, experimented with a choice program in which each public school instituted one of seven specialty programs and parents could enroll their children in any of the public schools.

While there are insights to be gained from such school choice systems, they are very limited in their application to vouchers. The alternative programs are generally designed and operated by the teachers and administrators who had run the district prior to the experiment. There are seldom opportunities for "outsiders" to bring new ideas or approaches to the fore. And everyone involved is generally employed and compensated according to whatever agreements were in place prior to the experiment. Because there are few tangible rewards for success—or penalties for failure—the effects of market pressures are considerably attenuated.

There have been only three true voucher experiments in U.S. schools: Indianapolis, Minneapolis, and Milwaukee have each implemented a very limited voucher plan within the last few years. The Indianapolis and Minneapolis programs are similar. Each is supported by a private corporation that provides small scholarships to low-income students who enroll in private schools, including religious schools. In both cases, the available funds limit participation to a few hundred students. The Indianapolis program currently provides scholarships of about $800 per student to about 1,000 students. One-half of the scholarships are reserved for students who had been enrolled in public schools. Up to one-half of the scholarships can go to students who had previously been enrolled in private schools. Applications have exceeded available scholarships by about 300 per year. In sum, roughly 500–800 students out of the nearly 50,000 students enrolled in Indianapolis public schools have chosen to participate in the program. The Minneapolis program is broadly similar in design, but smaller in all respects: smaller scholarships, fewer participants, shorter waiting lists, etc.

Milwaukee's program is state-supported. It provides vouchers of $2,738 (in 1992–93) to public school students who choose to switch to the private sector. Students must come from households with incomes 1.75 times the poverty line or less, and the students must have been enrolled in the Milwaukee public school system in the prior year. In addition, eligible private schools must have no religious affiliation and cannot charge the student more than the amount of the scholarship—both vital differences from California's current initiative.

Milwaukee public schools enroll about 90,000 students; about 60,000 are eligible to participate in the voucher program. To date, no independent high school has participated in the program. In effect, vouchers are available to the roughly 40,000 K–8 students currently enrolled in the public sector. Of those, 998 students, or roughly 2.5 percent, applied to private schools in 1992–93. Funding constraints limited participation to 613 students.

Observers of these programs agree that none has engendered significant changes in the public schools. That is hardly surprising; all three are so limited that they present little threat to the public sector. How many teachers or administrators would have been induced to change their thought patterns and behaviors by the loss of 1 or 2 percent of their district's students? The Milwaukee program does suggest that, at a minimum, private high schools were not provided the necessary incentive to provide education to public students at a price of roughly $2,700. But the restrictions on private schools and on student participation are considerably greater in the Milwaukee program than they are under the California initiative. Thus, it may hold few lessons for California.

THE PUBLIC SPENDING DEBATE

The debate over Proposition 174 has brought to the surface issues that have not been considered in detail in the prior discussions of the voucher concept. Specifically, Proposition 174's advocates argue that California faces a public finance crisis and the proposition will ease the burden of K–12 spending, freeing up funds for other uses. Its opponents argue that the proposition will result in devastating reductions in public school spending. Both sides present examples of the kinds of adverse effects California will experience if their position does not prevail, but neither side goes beyond limited examples.

The advocates' argument: California's school-age population is increasing rapidly. If public school enrollments continue to increase, simply maintaining current per-pupil spending levels would place increasing demands on the state's General Fund revenues. But because California has already severely slashed spending on most public services, finding these additional funds for K–12 education would be a serious concern. The proposition would help, they contend, because every departing student would cost the state only $2,600,[7] saving whatever the state would have spent on that student in the public schools—$4,200 by one estimate.[8]

Opponents argue that, for each student who transfers to a private school, required state spending on public schools will decrease by approximately twice the amount they otherwise would have received for that student—a "double hit" on state funding for K–12 education:

> The initiative reduces the overall state guarantee for funding K–12 education by approximately $4,500 for each student who leaves the public school system. Next, out of the remaining Proposition 98 funds, the state will take $2,500 to pay private school tuition. Then, by terms of the initiative the state is allowed to take credit for another $2,500 "savings" as though it had been spent on the schools.

---

[7]Although the legislature is free to set the value of the voucher, all commentaries, both advocating and opposing the proposition, assume the legislature will elect the minimum, half the amount spent per-public school pupil the previous year.

[8]David Barulich, "Model for Evaluating Fiscal Impact of Parental Choice in Education Proposition," unpublished paper, July 14, 1993. Barulich is one of Proposition 174's authors.

That's a $9,500 hit on public education funds for one student leaving the system.[9]

Neither side goes beyond such single-student examples to examine the full, systemwide implications of Proposition 174 for state spending on K–12 education.

THIS ANALYSIS

We have built a year-by-year simulation model of California's finance requirements under Propositions 98 and 111 and then incorporated the effects of Proposition 174 on these requirements. We explore the implications of alternative state spending policies and the controversy regarding the "double hit." This analysis has several limitations:

- We focus on the fiscal effects of Proposition 174 on the public school system—both total state costs and per-pupil spending in the public schools. Both advocates and opponents appear to agree that students who transfer to private schools have "voted with their feet" for a preferred alternative. Because such students, by their own judgment, are unambiguously better off, we do not concern ourselves with the finances and economics of the private sector.

- We consider the effects of the voucher initiative only on K–12 education. Propositions 98 and 111, the primary instruments defining California K–12 finance, also include community colleges. Some of the effects that we identify in this report will also affect the state's community college system. We ignore those issues.

- We analyze the effects of Proposition 174 on public K–12 spending at the state level. In fact, though, given the diversity of circumstances found in the districts across the state, 174's effects will likely affect public school districts in the state in different ways.

---

[9]Statement by Acting State Superintendent of Public Instruction William D. Dawson to the State Board of Education, California Department of Education, News Release Number 93-25, May 14, 1993.

- We focus on operational costs. If large numbers of students from overcrowded districts transfer to private schools, state spending for construction would probably be reduced.[10] Transfers out of school districts with excess capacity, on the other hand, will have a relatively low impact on capital needs in the future. In any event, this report ignores such effects.

THE ORGANIZATION OF THIS REPORT

Chapter Two analyzes the likely prospects for California's K–12 education finance without the voucher initiative. Chapter Three discusses those aspects of California's public finance system relevant to the voucher debate; it also describes the scenarios we will consider to explore the issues. Chapter Four presents our analysis of Proposition 174's effects on K–12 education finance in California. Finally, we summarize these effects in Chapter Five and discuss their implications.

---

[10]Construction costs for new schools average about $1,000 per pupil of capacity. The costs of construction vary significantly between districts and, in the large urban districts, between sites.

Chapter Two

PROSPECTS FOR CALIFORNIA K–12 EDUCATION WITHOUT VOUCHERS

To establish a baseline, we examine the future of K–12 financing in the state absent any significant policy changes. We begin with the two primary factors that will drive K–12 finance over the next decade—the state's demographics and economy—and then move on to the results of our analysis of the resulting K–12 finance scenario.

DEMOGRAPHIC TRENDS

Demographic trends are a major factor in determining the levels of expenditures on K–12 education under Propositions 98 and 111.[1] Table 2.1 presents the relevant population projections—total state population and public and private K–12 enrollments. These state population and K–12 enrollment projections are generally from the California Department of Finance (DoF),[2] although we amended the most recent DoF K–12 enrollment estimates to cover the entire time frame of our analysis.

---

[1]In this report we frequently refer to Propositions 98 and 111. Proposition 98, passed by the voters in 1988, laid out the framework for K–14 finance in California; hence, the minimum funding calculation for K–14 education is often called "Proposition 98 funding." In response to worsening economic conditions in the early 1990s, voters passed Proposition 111 in June 1990. Proposition 111 introduced a set of exceptions and qualifications to the rules initially imposed by Proposition 98. In combination, they define the framework for K–12 finance today, although the resulting funding level is still referred to as the "Proposition 98 guarantee."

[2]General population and K–12 enrollment series are unpublished series from the California Department of Finance Demographic Research Unit. Private enrollment series are derived in this analysis (see Appendix A).

Table 2.1

Demographic Trends in California, 1991–92 to 2002–03
(thousands)

	State Population	Public K–12 Enrollment	Private K–12 Enrollment
1991–92	30,646	5,002	545
1992–93	31,300	5,090	554
1993–94	31,906	5,172	556*
1994–95	32,520	5,294	561*
1995–96	33,188	5,456	571*
1996–97	33,963	5,656	582*
1997–98	34,524	5,871	593*
1998–99	35,182	6,094	605*
1999–00	35,824	6,321	616*
2000–01	36,443	6,553	626*
2001–02	37,044	6,782*	637*
2002–03	37,665	7,014*	648*

SOURCE: California Department of Finance, Demographic Research Unit.
* Estimates derived in this analysis.

California's population is expected to increase by 20 percent from approximately 31 million people in 1992–93 to nearly 38 million in 2002–03. While the growth in the state's overall population is large, the growth in the state's K–12 population is even greater, approaching 38 percent, from 5.6 million in 1992–93 to more than 7.7 million in 2002–03. Private enrollments are expected to remain flat over the next decade, rising only 17 percent from 554,000 in 1992–93 to 648,000 in 2002–03.

Because there is uncertainty in these estimates, a sensitivity analysis of our results for these demographic assumptions is presented in Appendix H. The methodology for bounding the inputs to this sensitivity analysis is given in Appendix A.

THE STATE ECONOMY AND BUDGET

Another primary determinant of the levels of public expenditures on K–12 education is the state's economic condition. Forecasting the state's economy is difficult. Even the state recognizes the difficulty of such an effort. The Commission on State Finance, the agency responsible for providing these estimates, recently reduced its projection window from ten years to a mere two years.

We developed our own estimates of the relevant state and local tax revenues through 2002–03. The methodology and details for this model are given in Appendix B. Table 2.2 shows our projections for the two most crucial drivers of the state's K–12 finance formula— General Fund revenues and K–12 local property taxes. We also developed projections of the other monies that funnel into K–12 education—federal funds, lottery revenues, and miscellaneous other local revenues. These methodologies and the resulting series are included in Appendix C.

General Fund revenues are projected to grow from $42 billion in 1991–92 to $64 billion in 2002–03, while local K–12 property taxes[3]

Table 2.2

**General Fund Revenues and K–12 Local
Property Taxes, 1991–92 to 2002–03
(billions of dollars)**

	General Fund Revenues	K–12 Local Property Taxes
1991–92	42.0	5.6
1992–93	41.0	6.7
1993–94	39.5	9.0
1994–95	41.5	9.2
1995–96	43.6	9.5
1996–97	44.8	9.8
1997–98	47.0	10.3
1998–99	49.4	10.7
1999–00	52.3	11.3
2000–01	55.5	11.9
2001–02	59.4	12.6
2002–03	63.5	13.4

SOURCE: This analysis, see Appendix B.

---

[3]As noted above, we are focusing on K–12 in this analysis. Accordingly, any local property tax numbers and Proposition 98 minimum funding guarantees refer only to the portion associated with K–12. See Appendix D for a further discussion of our assumptions regarding the breakdown between K–12 and community college funding.

grow from $5.6 billion to $13.4 billion over the same period.[4] These two series represent the general pool of state-controlled resources from which K–12 education can draw. In contrast to the state's last long-term projection of the state economy (issued before the current state economic downturn in 1991), which anticipated an average annual growth rate of 7.0 percent for the 1991 to 2001 period,[5] our analysis projects a modest 3.5 percent average annual growth rate.

Note that the property tax stream in Table 2.2 represents only those available to K–12. Because this analysis concentrates on the effects of the voucher initiative on K–12 finance, the property taxes presented reflect only those allocated to K–12 education. We assume that the state will not continue its recent pattern of diverting an increasing share of overall local property taxes from cities, counties, and special districts to schools. The detailed methodology for these projections is included in Appendix C.

In recognition of the tremendous uncertainty associated with these estimates, we performed a test of the sensitivity of our results to these estimates; that test is presented in Appendix H. The methodology for determining the bounds of this sensitivity analysis for General Fund revenues is included in Appendix B and for K–12 local property taxes in Appendix C.

FUNDING OF K–12 EDUCATION

K–12 finance in California is governed by a complex set of rules that were implemented by the voters in November 1988 as Proposition 98 and amended in June 1990 by Proposition 111.[6] These two propositions, incorporated into Article XVI of the State Constitution, lay out the complex framework for the minimum amount to be funded for K–12 education.

---

[4]Note that the increases for fiscal years 1992–93 and 1993–94 include state transfers of local property taxes from cities, counties, and special districts totaling $1.3 billion and $2.6 billion, respectively.

[5]Commission on State Finance (COSF), *1991 Annual Long-Term General Fund Forecast*, Fall 1991, Table 2, p. 19.

[6]This legislation actually refers to K–14 education funding. To simplify this analysis, we will convert all K–14 references and values to appropriate K–12 values. See Appendix D for details.

The rules controlling K–12 finance in California separate years into two categories—those years when the per-capita General Fund revenues grow as fast or faster than inflation (as measured by the growth in per-capita personal income) and those years when it grows more slowly.

In high-growth years, the minimum level of K–12 funding is determined by the greater of either Test One or Test Two. **Test One** is calculated as a predetermined percentage of overall General Fund revenues.[7] **Test Two** requires that the real per-pupil state and local property tax expenditures at least equal that of the prior year.[8]

In low-growth years, minimum per-capita K–12 education state and local property tax expenditures are governed by Test Three, which requires that they change at the same rate as the per-capita General Fund revenues, plus 0.5 percent. Another provision of the education code in Test Three years requires that K–12 education fare no worse than all other spending categories of the General Fund combined.

K–12 FINANCE PROSPECTS: A BASELINE FOR COMPARISON

Given the demographic and economic projections presented earlier, the minimum funding levels for K–12 education under Propositions 98 and 111 are shown in Table 2.3. The first column lists state and local support for K–12 education. This total includes all General Fund expenditures on K–12 education and local property taxes allocated to K–12 education. It is an aggregate measure of the cost to the state of providing K–12 education to its residents and does not include lottery funds or nonproperty tax local support to K–12 education. These quantities are allocated separately for specific purposes.

The second column in Table 2.3 lists the total resources available, per pupil, to the public K–12 school system. These funds include federal

---

[7]It was originally equal to the K–14 share of the 1986–87 budget or about 40 percent. This number has been adjusted to reflect the recent transfers of property taxes to K–14 from other uses, and is about 33 percent in 1993–94.

[8]This is accomplished by adjusting the prior year's Proposition 98 spending by the change in enrollments and inflation.

Table 2.3

Minimum K–12 Funding Without Vouchers, 1991–92 to 2002–03

	State and Local Support for K–12 Education (billions of 1993 dollars)	Total Resources Per Public School Pupil (1993 dollars per pupil)	K–12 Education's Share of General Fund Revenues (in percent)
1991–92	22.69	5,422	38
1992–93	22.03	5,272	36
1993–94	21.70	5,125	32
1994–95	22.22	5,156	33
1995–96	22.92	5,186	34
1996–97	23.28	5,119	35
1997–98	24.23	5,149	36
1998–99	25.18	5,170	37
1999–00	26.40	5,235	39
2000–01	27.71	5,307	40
2001–02	29.32	5,424	41
2002–03	30.98	5,545	43

funds, lottery funds, and other local income funds, in addition to state General Fund revenues and local property taxes. This is a measure of the total pool of resources available to public schools. The third column presents the share of total General Fund revenues committed to K–12 education under the rules of Propositions 98 and 111.

Note that for the purposes of this and all subsequent discussions in this report, the results are given in constant 1993 dollars. We have used a conservative 3 percent inflation rate to deflate dollars over time.[9] A more detailed justification of this assumption is included in Appendix D. In addition, we performed a sensitivity analysis of this assumption; that analysis is presented in Appendix H.

As Table 2.3 shows, minimum spending on K–12 education will grow rapidly over the next decade from $22 billion[10] in 1992–93 to $31 billion in 2002–03, a 41 percent increase. Under current law, private

---

[9]This rate is also used by the state for similar purposes.

[10]Note that these are constant dollars, assuming a 3 percent rate of inflation.

schools receive an inconsequential share of these monies; effectively, all state and local property tax funds are expended on public K–12. Total per-pupil resources will remain relatively flat, rising only 5 percent from $5,272 in 1992–93 to $5,545 in 2002–03.

The share of total General Fund revenues that must be allocated to K–12 education will grow rapidly through 2002–03, rising from 32 percent in 1993–94 to 43 percent in 2002–03.[11]

This rise is problematic for the state, however, and is an important factor in the current debate. In 1993–94, more than two-thirds of all General Fund expenditures are "mandated state spending." These funds are controlled by state constitutional measures, such as Propositions 98 and 111, and by federal law, and their levels are not subject to the legislature's discretion. This leaves less than one-third of the state's General Fund revenues for those agencies that have no federally or constitutionally mandated spending levels, such as state police, higher education, and corrections.   If K–12's mandated spending share increases by 11 percent over the next ten years, the discretionary share must decrease by the same amount, forcing debilitating cutbacks in those key agencies. The state is facing a serious fiscal crisis. Voucher proponents argue that the initiative is needed to decrease net demands on the state's resources and to mitigate this crisis.

SUMMARY

State and local K–12 expenditures on education under Propositions 98 and 111 are expected to rise 41 percent in real terms over the next decade while real per-student resources in public schools remain relatively flat. The growth in cost results from the anticipated rapid growth in K–12 enrollments during the period.

K–12 expenditures as a share of total General Fund revenues are expected to increase from 32 percent in 1993–94 to 43 percent in

---

[11]Lawrence Picus, in his article "An Update on California School Finance 1992–93: What Does the Future Hold?" *Journal of Education Finance*, Fall 1992, pp. 142–162, predicts a K–12 share of 48 percent of General Fund revenues by 2001–02.

2002–03. This increase in K–12 education's mandated share of General Fund revenues will likely precipitate or at least accelerate a crisis in the state's fiscal architecture.

Chapter Three

PROPOSITION 174: KEY ISSUES AND POSSIBLE SCENARIOS

The impact of the voucher initiative on California's fiscal environment at both the state and public school levels hinges on three factors: (1) the existence or nonexistence of a "double hit" on public K–12 finance through the initiative; (2) the magnitude of the shift of current and prospective public K–12 students to private schools; and (3) the range of K–12 funding alternatives the state can elect to pursue under the voucher initiative.

THE EXISTENCE OF A DOUBLE HIT

Section 17, subdivision (b), paragraph (8) of Proposition 174 states:

(8) Expenditures for scholarships issued under this Section and savings[1] resulting from implementation of this Section shall count toward the minimum funding requirements for education established by Sections 8 and 8.5 of Article XVI. Students enrolled in scholarship-redeeming schools shall not be counted toward enrollment in public schools and community colleges for purposes of Sections 8 and 8.5 of Article XVI.

It includes two provisions: (1) state expenditures for scholarships and "savings" will count toward the Proposition 98 minimum expenditure on K–12 education and (2) students who attend scholarship-redeeming schools instead of public schools will not count to-

---

[1] "Savings" is explicitly defined in Proposition 174 as the number of scholarship students times average spending per pupil in the public schools less the scholarship.

17

ward the Proposition 98 formulas. This passage has given rise to the debate over the so-called "double hit."

Proponents and opponents of the voucher initiative agree that only the first provision is relevant in years when Test One of Proposition 98 is determinative. If the minimum state guarantee to K–12 is determined by a preset share of total General Fund revenues, the second provision, reducing the number of students counted in determining the state's obligation under Test Two, would have no effect. The resulting level of funding guaranteed to *public* schools would then be the Proposition 98 guarantee amount under Test One less expenditures for scholarships and "savings."

The debate, however, arises over years in which the state budget process falls under Tests Two and Three of Propositions 98 and 111. In these years, the minimum guarantee is the product of the prior year's expenditure on K–12 education times a budget multiplier (either the inflation rate or the change in per-capita General Fund revenues) and adjusted for the change in enrollments. When the second provision of paragraph (8) of the initiative is applied, therefore, the Proposition 98 guarantee decreases for each student who leaves the public school system. If the first provision is also applied, as many opponents to the initiative argue, then the expenditures on scholarships and "savings" are counted against this already-reduced amount—ergo the double hit.

Proponents of the initiative argue that these two provisions are intended to interact individually with Proposition 98 and that there will be no double hit. They argue that the first provision is intended to apply in years when the state budget falls under Test One and the second provision when the state budget falls under Tests Two and Three.

Because there is nothing in the initiative to resolve the ambiguity over this issue, we are unable to provide a resolution to this debate. Subsequently, we analyze both scenarios in this report.

THE MAGNITUDE OF THE SHIFT FROM PUBLIC TO PRIVATE SCHOOLS

The students who shift from the public sector to the private sector are both a source of savings to the taxpayers of the state and a source of lost revenues to the public sector. Shift, in the context of this analysis, refers to the students who, absent vouchers, would attend public schools, but because of the voucher initiative attend scholarship-redeeming schools. The magnitude of this shift is one of the most crucial determinants of the prospective effects of the voucher initiative.

The available data are not sufficient to assess the magnitude of this shift. The Milwaukee, Indianapolis, and Minneapolis experiments are so small in their application that they provide little information on the likely shift under the California voucher initiative. The number of applications for participation in the voucher programs in Milwaukee, Indianapolis, and Minneapolis has been less than 4 percent of those who are eligible to participate, possibly suggesting the potential for a small shift under a voucher program in California. However, all three voucher programs are considerably more restrictive on participation in the program both by students and by private schools. Given the small shifts experienced in each of these programs, it is difficult to know whether it was the constraints or simply limited interest in a voucher program.

Another factor that complicates estimating the magnitude of the shift is the likely constitutional challenge to the distribution of public monies to religious schools. Parochial and religious schools are likely to play a key role in any scenario that results in a large shift of students out of the public schools. A ruling that disallows the distribution of state monies to these schools in the form of scholarships would likely dampen the size of the shift.

We examine, therefore, two scenarios that represent general bounds on the magnitude of shifts in the current public debate. We use these levels not to endorse or validate their actual values, but to explore what might happen under what appear to be the extreme cases.

For the "high-shift" scenario, we have chosen a shift of 34 percent of current and prospective K–12 enrollments. This shift, in addition to the market share private schools would have regardless of vouchers, would result in the 40 percent market share proposed by the voucher initiative's proponents.[2]

For the lower bound, we have chosen one of the most conservative estimates proposed in the public debate, a shift rate of only 4 percent, as described in a recent study by the Southwest Regional Laboratory.[3] That study surveyed existing private schools and attempted to assess the extent to which they would be willing to expand their capacities in response to the voucher proposal. While the specifics of the study have been the subject of debate, the 4 percent shift represents the lower bound in the public discourse.

THE RANGE OF STATE POLICY CHOICES

Proposition 98 represents only a floor to state spending. In fact, recent history has shown that the state is willing to fund K–12 education at levels in excess of the Proposition 98 guarantee. In both the 1992–93 and 1993–94 fiscal years, when the state's General Fund revenues contracted and kicked the state into a Test Three world, the K–12 budget was supplemented with additional "non-Proposition 98 funding loans" to supplement the guarantee funding floor. The general rule, in these two instances, has been to maintain a constant (in nominal terms) level of per-pupil public funding.[4]

There is some controversy, however, about whether such loans, spent on K–12 education, can be excluded from the Proposition 98 definition of state and local expenditures on K–12 education. It can be argued that since these amounts were used to fund state-supported K–12 education activities, they represent expenditures on

---

[2]David Barulich, "Savings Could Exceed Cost of School Voucher Program," *The Los Angeles Times*, July 22, 1993, p. A1.

[3]Marcella R. Dianda and Ronald G. Corwin, *What a Voucher Could Buy: A Survey of California's Private Schools*, Southwest Regional Laboratory, February 1993, p. 17.

[4]It is important to recognize, however, that while this may have been the policy in the past, it does not guarantee a continuation of this approach in the future. Some argue, for example, that K–12 education has been isolated from the impacts of the reduced state resources and that perhaps its turn to take the hit is coming next.

K–12 education and should be included in the base amount for the next year's Proposition 98 calculation.[5] Because our objective in this analysis is to bound the possible fiscal impacts of the voucher initiative on the state and public education, the outcome of this controversy does not directly counteract any of our conclusions. It would complicate the final interpretation of our results as future options and opportunities for action would be progressively constrained by current and future policy decisions.

It is important to keep in mind that if spending the Proposition 98 minimum under Proposition 174 would result in sudden and harsh reductions in the level of state support for the public school system, it is possible that the state would increase its spending over this floor amount to mitigate the negative effects of the initiative. In general, the legislature could pursue a whole range of options in implementing Proposition 174 and in funding K–12 education.

In the course of this analysis, we will focus on four such scenarios that we believe represent a reasonable range of the policy options available to the state. It is important to remember, however, that these scenarios are not exhaustive and that the state could choose spending policies beyond those we analyze.

Minimum Funding. In this scenario, the state spends the minimum it can under Propositions 98 and 111. This scenario represents the lower bound of the decision space for the state. California is constitutionally bound to provide at least the Proposition 98 level of funding. In this scenario, under those circumstances when the Proposition 98 minimum budget is offset by Proposition 174 "savings," the state chooses not to spend those savings on K–12 education. This scenario represents the minimum the state can fund whether there is a double hit or not.

Full Budget. In this scenario, the state chooses to remain true to the spirit of Proposition 98 and spend the entire Proposition 98 budget on K–12 education, notwithstanding Proposition 174's offset of "savings" against the Proposition 98 budget. Since this scenario requires the expenditure of the savings, it can occur only if the legislature's

---

[5]A lawsuit on this issue is currently in litigation in the Sacramento Superior Court (*CTA v. Russell Gould,* File No. 373415).

K–12 appropriation exceeds the Proposition 98 guarantee by an amount sufficient to offset the savings reduction.

Maintain State Effort. This scenario assumes that the state spends as much under vouchers as it would have spent if the voucher initiative had been defeated. K–12 education spending is first calculated as if vouchers were not implemented. The cost of the expected scholarships is then deducted from this amount and the balance is allocated to public education. This scenario is not likely if the state continues its progress into a fiscal crisis.

Hold Harmless. In this scenario, the state essentially continues its current policy of holding the per-pupil total expenditure on public K–12 education constant over time or "holding public students harmless" with regard to the effects of the voucher initiative. In this scenario, the state is assumed to maintain the total per-pupil expenditure on public education at the same level as described in the baseline scenario in Chapter Two.[6]

---

[6]While this approach maintains a constant *total* per-pupil spending level in public schools, it is not the same as maintaining constant *state* per-pupil spending. Non-Proposition 98 funding of K–12 education is often categorical and constrained to specific student populations. For example, federal subsidies for special education students can be spent only on these students. Implicit in our analysis, therefore, is an assumption that these students remain in public schools.

Chapter Four

THE EFFECTS OF VOUCHERS ON PUBLIC EXPENDITURES FOR K–12 EDUCATION

The Parental Choice in Education Act is likely to have profound implications for K–12 finance in California. To frame the analysis of this complex issue, we have added the provisions of the voucher initiative to our Proposition 98 model. In addition, we have added provisions for the four scenarios in the previous chapter, as well as a sensitivity test for the presence of a double hit. These provisions were added to assess their effects on Proposition 98 and K–12 education finance. The mechanics and details of this model are provided in Appendix E. Note that the assumptions bounding this stage of the analysis are also discussed in detail in Appendix E.

The findings of our analysis will be described along four axes: over time, whether there is a double hit, whether the magnitude of the shift is high or low, and across the four policy scenarios detailed in the prior chapter. Because the results varied significantly between the high- and low-shift scenarios, we will consider the results under each of these scenarios separately at first and then with the two put together.

We will analyze the outcomes in each scenario along two key dimensions—the level of resources available per pupil[1] to the public schools and the amount it will cost the state to provide K–12 education to its residents. The first dimension is a measure of the "financial health" of the public schools. We measure this by tracking the total level of

---

[1] Using total resources available to public schools would not capture the effects of serving a smaller student population. Accordingly, we assess the outcomes in terms of per-pupil levels of resources in public schools.

resources (state, local property taxes, federal, lottery, and other sources) available per student in the public schools.

The second outcome measure is total state and local support for K–12 education. This measure includes both the public sector costs (General Fund revenues and local property taxes) and public expenditures on private schools (scholarships); it reflects the demands of K–12 education on the state's fiscal resources.

K–12 ENROLLMENTS UNDER ALTERNATIVE-SHIFT SCENARIOS

The number of students in the public and private sectors under both the low- and high-shift scenarios is given in Table 4.1. The shift in each case represents the fraction of students who, absent vouchers, would have attended public schools but, under vouchers, attend scholarship-redeeming schools. We assume the total shift is phased in linearly over an eight-year period. Under a 4 percent scenario, for example, 0.5 percent will shift the first year, 1.0 percent the second year, 1.5 percent the third year, until in year eight (and thereafter) 4 percent of the public students are attending private schools.

Without vouchers, the baseline public enrollments increase 38 percent from 1992–93 to 2002–03, while private enrollments increase 17 percent. Private schools account for just over 8 percent of all enrollments in 2002–03. Under a 4 percent (low-shift) scenario, public schools are only slightly affected, growing at 32 percent, while private school enrollments grow at a blazing 68 percent, ending up with a 12 percent market share in 2002–03. In the 34 percent (high-shift) scenario, public school enrollments decline by 9 percent, while private enrollments explode, growing 447 percent over the decade and ending with a 40 percent market share in 2002–03.

In the baseline case, the world without vouchers, Test Two of Proposition 98 is generally the operative test, as the growth in K–12 enrollments far outstrips General Fund revenue growth. The only variation is in 1995–96, when the surtax on wealthier taxpayers expires and General Fund revenues grow slowly enough to trigger Test Three.

Since the low-shift scenario does not affect public enrollments very much, the operative tests remain the same as in the baseline. In the

Table 4.1

Projected K–12 Enrollments Under Alternative-Shift Scenarios (thousands of students)

	Public K–12 Enrollments		
	Baseline	4% Shift	34% Shift
1991–92	5,002*	5,002*	5,002*
1992–93	5,090*	5,090*	5,090*
1993–94	5,172	5,146	4,952
1994–95	5,294	5,241	4,844
1995–96	5,456	5,374	4,760
1996–97	5,656	5,543	4,694
1997–98	5,871	5,724	4,623
1998–99	6,094	5,911	4,540
1999–00	6,321	6,100	4,441
2000–01	6,553	6,291	4,325
2001–02	6,782	6,511	4,476
2002–03	7,014	6,733	4,629
	Private K–12 Enrollments		
	Baseline	4% Shift	34% Shift
1991–92	545*	545*	545*
1992–93	554*	554*	554*
1993–94	556	582	776
1994–95	561	614	1,011
1995–96	571	653	1,267
1996–97	582	695	1,544
1997–98	593	740	1,840
1998–99	605	788	2,159
1999–00	616	837	2,496
2000–01	626	888	2,854
2001–02	637	908	2,943
2002–03	648	928	3,032

SOURCES: California Department of Finance and this analysis.

* Indicates actual number. See Appendix A for detailed information on sources.

high-shift scenario, however, the shifts in enrollments are large
enough to make Test One the operative test in 1995–96, 1997–98,
1998–99, 1999–00, and 2000–01.

K–12 FINANCE UNDER A DOUBLE-HIT INTERPRETATION

Under the double-hit interpretation, spending on scholarships and
the amount of the "savings" count toward the Proposition 98 guarantee in all budget scenarios.

The Effects of a Low Shift

Since we are in a Test Two world during the majority of the decade
under the 4 percent shift assumption, the double-hit assumption
generally affects the outcomes in our scenarios. Figure 4.1 presents
the total resources the state is expected to spend under each of the
policy scenarios described in the previous chapter.

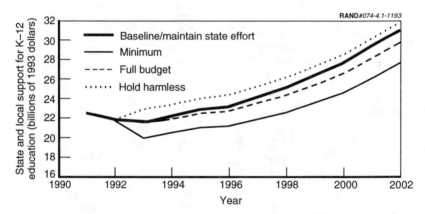

NOTE: There is a nonzero origin on the y-axis. This has been done to
facilitate the discussion of the implications of the different policies and to make
the differences easier to evaluate. Unless otherwise noted, we have used the
same scale on the axes of the figures. For example, this figure has the same
scale as Figure 4.4 and Figure 4.7.

**Figure 4.1—State and Local Support for K–12 Education: Double Hit,
4 Percent Shift**

The dark solid line ("Baseline") represents the baseline level of spending presented in Chapter Two. It is our estimate of what the state will spend on K–12 education in accordance with Propositions 98 and 111 if the voucher initiative is defeated. The lighter solid line ("Minimum") represents the minimum level of K–12 spending under the double-hit interpretation of Proposition 174. Note that this line does not plot the Proposition 98 minimum, but total state spending under the Proposition 98 minimum condition (the amount spent by the state on public schools plus the amount spent on scholarships). The "Minimum" line lies below the "Baseline" as savings count toward the Proposition 98 guarantee, reducing the amount of spending necessary to comply with the guarantee.[2]

The dashed "Full Budget" line represents the state spending if it chooses to spend the Proposition 174 "savings" on public K–12 education. The "Full Budget" line, which represents reinvesting the savings under the proposition back into public K–12 education, starts off coincident with the "Baseline" but then gradually diverges. This divergence reflects the eventual stepping down of the total Proposition 98 guarantee because of the decreasing enrollments. The difference between the "Minimum" and "Full Budget" lines represents the savings, as defined by Proposition 174.

Since "Maintain State Effort" is, by definition, a policy in which the state spends the same amount on K–12 as it would under the "Baseline" scenario, it coincides with the "Baseline."

The dotted "Hold Harmless" line represents a policy whereby the state increases spending to hold public per-pupil spending at the same level as would have occurred under the baseline. The "Hold Harmless" line rises above the "Baseline" and moves parallel to it, reflecting the increased state expenditure necessary to hold public per-pupil spending constant as the nonpublic expenditure on scholarships carves into the funding available to public schools.

Figure 4.2 shows the effects of the voucher initiative, assuming a 4 percent shift and a double hit, on total spending per pupil in the public schools. Public school per-capita spending will generally de-

---

[2]Since the diagram plots *all* public support of K–12 education, the cost of the scholarships is included in the spending shown.

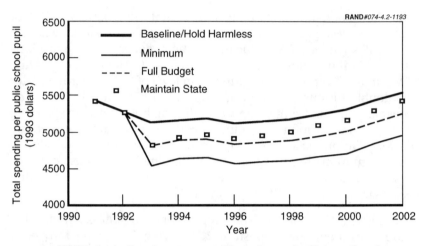

NOTE: Again, there is a nonzero origin on the y-axis. Unless otherwise noted, we have used the same scale on the axes of the figures. For example, this figure has the same scale as Figure 4.5 and Figure 4.8.

Figure 4.2—Total Spending Per Public School Pupil: Double Hit, 4 Percent Shift

crease relative to the "Baseline" in all scenarios except the "Hold Harmless" scenario, which by definition keeps this value the same as that of the "Baseline." The force driving this effect is that the expenditures on scholarships, including payments for students who previously received no money, displace some of the funds that would otherwise have been available for public students. Absent an actual increase in the state's overall spending on K–12 education, this displacement causes a reduction in public per-pupil spending.

One useful way to understand the differential impacts of the voucher initiative is to create a summary measure of its impacts across time in the various scenarios. Figure 4.3 presents such a summary, using average values over the decade to plot the initiative's effects.

Figure 4.3 plots the average over time for each of the series in Figures 4.1 and 4.2 against each other. It shows how the range of options we have identified works overall when compared to the baseline. The x-axis shows the total state expenditures on K–12 education—which was the y-axis in Figure 4.1—representing the cost to the state of

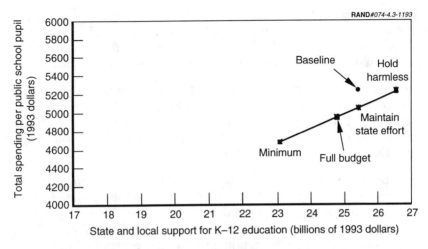

NOTE: There are nonzero origins on both axes. All of the policy space diagrams use the same scales on the axes for comparability, unless otherwise noted.

Figure 4.3—Policy Space: Double Hit, 4 Percent Shift

providing K–12 education under each of the alternative scenarios. Similarly, the y-axis represents total spending on public education per public pupil—the y-axis from Figure 4.2. This is a measure of the resources available to public schools under the scenario.

Hence, the point labeled "Baseline" represents the average of the "Baseline" series along each of the two axes, and each of the other points shown reflects the averages of the respective series over time. We have connected the scenarios to represent the fact that the state can choose to spend not only at the levels of the scenarios we have presented but also at intermediate levels in between. For example, if the state chose to spend half of the "savings" arising from the voucher initiative, the resulting policy point would fall approximately halfway between the "Full Spending" and "Minimum" points on Figure 4.3.

Since these actual numbers are sensitive to the various assumptions about the model's inputs, the utility of this diagram lies in the way it defines the relationships between the policy choices. Policy choices below the "Baseline" on this graph indicate that public schools, on average, receive fewer dollars per student over the course of the decade than would be expected absent vouchers.[3] Policy choices to the left of the "Baseline" reflect scenarios where the state will spend less than it would have, absent vouchers, to fund K–12 education.

Average real per-pupil spending over the next decade, under the assumptions in this scenario, will be about $5,242. Similarly, real state "Baseline" spending will average about $25.4 billion. The "Minimum" value in this scenario is estimated at $4,643 per public pupil and $22.8 billion in state spending.

The policy alternatives under this scenario generally fall on a line below the baseline point. For example, to reach the baseline level of per-pupil public spending ("Hold Harmless"), the state must increase its average spending on K–12 education from $25.4 billion to $26.5 billion—a 4.3 increase in spending levels. If the state wishes to hold spending at baseline levels, it must be willing to accept a corresponding reduction in per-pupil public K–12 spending from an average of $5,242 to $5,048 per student—a 3.8 percent decrease. These results hold only for the assumptions of this scenario—a 4 percent shift and a double hit.

The Effects of a High Shift

The public expenditure scenario for K–12 education under a 34 percent shift and a double hit is presented in Figure 4.4.

The large shift of students to the private sector results in a significant decrease in the "Minimum" real K–12 education demands, as defined by Propositions 98 and 111, on state and local resources, falling from $21 billion in 1992–93 to only $18 billion in 2002–03. It is important to remember that these expenditures include both the state General Funds and local property taxes spent on public K–12 education as well as the public General Funds spent on scholarships.

The "Full Spending" scenario results in a higher level of state spending, but one that is generally below the "Baseline" scenario without

---

[3]This is based on the Proposition 98 guarantee. Given the fiscal crisis facing the state, reaching these spending levels is also uncertain.

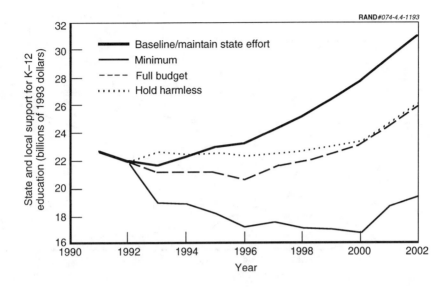

Figure 4.4—State and Local Support for K–12 Education: Double Hit,
34 Percent Shift

vouchers. The difference between the "Minimum" line and the "Full Spending" line represents the "savings" as they are defined in Proposition 174. The "Hold Harmless" spending scenario, in which the per-pupil public school expenditure is held at "Baseline" levels, initially rises above the "Baseline" as current private students suddenly become eligible for scholarships and then drops below the "Baseline" as the state realizes savings from fully supporting fewer public students.

Turning to the effects of the various policies on total resources per public pupil to the public schools under a 34 percent shift and no double hit, we arrive at Figure 4.5. Per pupil, we can see that public schools would receive a much lower level of support if the state chose to fund at the Proposition 98 guarantee level. Much of the ground lost by public schools would be made up, however, if the state chose to spend the "savings" under Proposition 174 on public K–12 education, as shown by the "Full Budget" line. The "Hold

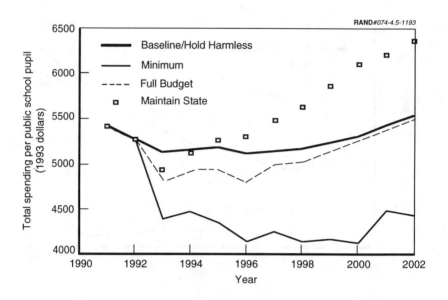

**Figure 4.5—Total Spending Per Public School Pupil: Double Hit,
34 Percent Shift**

Harmless" scenario is, by definition, equal to the "Baseline" spending, while the "Maintain State Effort" result would substantially increase resources to public schools as the state spent a constant level of money on fewer public and less-expensive private students.

Placing these results in the context of our summary "Policy Space," we arrive at Figure 4.6. Note that the line in this figure is generally above and to the left of the baseline point.

Again, each point in Figure 4.6 represents the average over the decade of the series shown in Figures 4.4 and 4.5. The "Minimum," representing the minimum commitment to K–12 education that the state can make under these assumptions, is much lower than the nonvoucher spending (lies to the left of the "Baseline") and provides a much lower level of resources to the public schools (lies below the "Baseline"). The "Full Spending" scenario moves closer to the nonvoucher result but still falls short in both dimensions. The "Hold Harmless" approach attains nonvoucher levels of spending at a

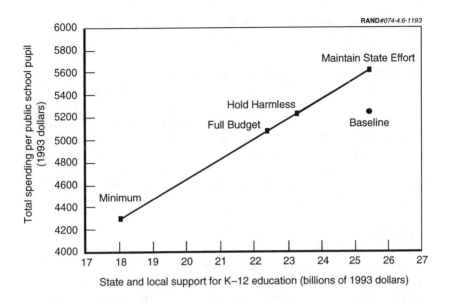

Figure 4.6—Policy Space: Double Hit, 34 Percent Shift

much lower cost to the state, while the "Maintain State Effort" scenario yields a much higher level of spending for the public schools.

In general, the savings realized in the high-shift scenario from moving public students to less-expensive private schools produce a wide range of financial opportunities to the state, as the policy scenarios generally lie on a line above and to the left of the "Baseline." The state, for example, can spend the "Baseline" $25.5 billion and increase average annual public per-pupil resources to $5,630, or the state can fund public K–12 at the same levels as in the "Baseline" and save an average of $2.2 billion, or 8.6 percent. Herein lies the savings that voucher proponents tout as one way to address the state's fiscal crisis.

The combination of the high shift and double hit in this scenario significantly reduces the mandated level of spending on public K–12 education. Note that in this scenario, while the public per-pupil resources under the Proposition 98 "Minimum" scenario fall to a mere $4,300 per student, an 18 percent decrease in real resources, the total state and local expenditure on K–12 education decreases an average of $7.4 billion a year.

K–12 FINANCE UNDER A NO-DOUBLE-HIT INTERPRETATION

The alternative interpretation of the double hit is that spending on scholarships and the amount of the "savings" count toward the Proposition 98 guarantee only in years when the minimum guarantee is determined by Test One of Proposition 98. Otherwise, the scholarships are simply another (additional) cost to the state and the "savings" are ignored.

The Effects of a Low Shift

Under the no-double-hit assumption, public K–12 education receives the full amount of the Proposition 98 guarantee, and the cost of the scholarships is additional and separate to the state. We have presented the total state and local support for education in Figure 4.7.

It is important to remember that this support represents claims on the state's resources and includes the total cost to the state of providing K–12 education to its population, including state expenditures on public K–12 education, K–12 local property taxes, and expenditures on scholarships.

The result of the no-double-hit scenario is quite straightforward. There is in effect only *one* series—the "Minimum"—because the other policy alternatives all fall below the line denoting the Proposition 98 minimum. It is important to remember in this scenario that this line represents the Proposition 98 guarantee for the public schools *plus* the cost of the scholarships for those students not in the public sector.

Figure 4.8 shows the effects of the low-shift, no-double-hit scenario on the public school system (as measured by total per-pupil resources).

Note that the Minimum scenario provides more funding per public pupil than the Baseline scenario, even in a no-double-hit world. This

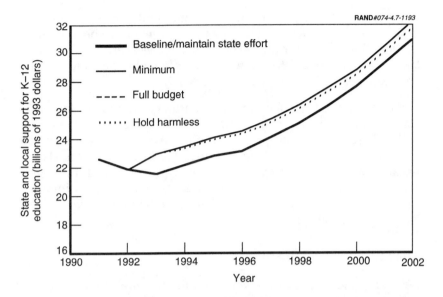

**Figure 4.7—State and Local Support for K–12 Education: No Double Hit,
4 Percent Shift**

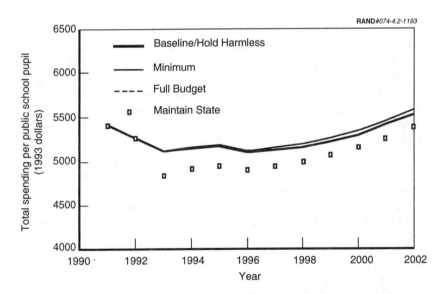

**Figure 4.8—Total Spending Per Public School Pupil: No Double Hit,
4 Percent Shift**

is because 16 to 20 percent of the public funds overall come from nonstate sources. When these resources, which have been retained in the public sector for purposes of this analysis, are divided over a smaller number of public school students, a higher per-pupil level of spending results.[4]

Figure 4.9 shows the policy space that arises from the no-double-hit assumption in the low-shift scenario. As can be seen from this diagram, there is only one policy option and it requires a 4 percent increase in state and local expenditures on K–12 education. This is because all of the other spending policies we analyze in this report require spending less than or equal to that spent in the "Minimum" scenario. Therefore, the range of state spending policy choices collapses into a single point.

The Effects of a High Shift

Reviewing the results of the voucher initiative under the high shift, the no-double-hit assumption produces a different and interesting set of implications. Figure 4.10 presents the first of these results, state and local support for K–12 education under this scenario.

The no-double-hit interpretation of the voucher initiative would result in several large shifts and swings in the minimum state and local support for K–12 education. These discontinuities result from a combination of three factors: (1) under the no-double-hit interpretation of Proposition 174, scholarships and savings are counted toward the Proposition 98 minimum in years in which Test One is in effect, but not in years when Test Two or Three is in effect; (2) the large shift of students to the private sector introduces the possibility that transitions and oscillations between Tests One and Two (or Three) will occur; and (3) a given year's scholarship amount is a function of the prior year's public per-pupil expenditure on K–12 education. The interactions and dynamics themselves are complex and explained in detail in Appendix I. The bottom line is that they do oc-

_____

[4]As noted earlier, this assumption also has implications as to the distributability of that money to not-categorical students. The levels of discretionary money available to these schools could dwindle rapidly. Since we assume that all of the categorical students remain in public schools, these effects may be minimized in our model. If these students leave the public schools, it will increase the burden on the state to sustain the total per-pupil funding in public schools.

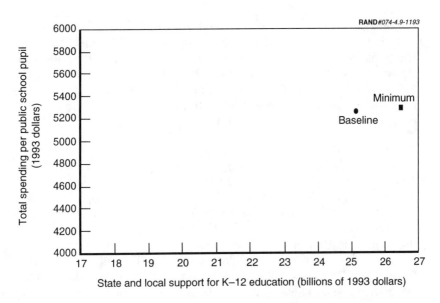

Figure 4.9—Policy Space: No Double Hit, 4 Percent Shift

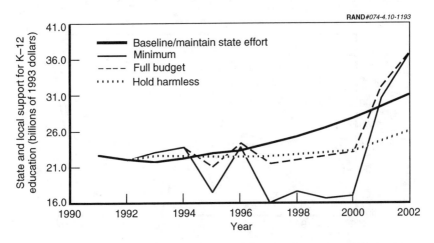

NOTE: The y-axis scale on this figure differs from the scale on Figures 4.1, 4.4, and 4.7. This reflects the wider variability associated with the shocks described in the analysis of this figure.

Figure 4.10—State and Local Support for K–12 Education: No Double Hit, 34 Percent Shift

cur and can result in major shifts—both in the level of funding the state is obligated to provide under Propositions 98 and 111, and in the total levels of per-pupil resources available to public schools (as shown in Figure 4.11). Note that these shocks occur only in the "Minimum" and "Full Budget" spending scenarios. If the state chooses to spend at a level higher than that of the Proposition 98 budget, then the shocks are not encountered.

These shifts are large, including a downward shift of $8.8 billion (26 percent) in the Proposition 98 guarantee from 1994–95 to 1995–96, an upward shift of $6.3 billion (35 percent) from 1995–96 to 1996–97, a downward shift of $7.7 billion (32 percent) from 1996–97 to 1997–98, and a $13.6 billion increase (80 percent) from 2000–01 to 2001–02. The first pair of shifts, between 1994–95 and 1996–97, is sensitive to the economic assumptions in our model: They disappear in the low-growth test case of our sensitivity analysis. The other large shift, from 1996–97 through 2000–01, however, was robust across all of the sensitivity tests. These shifts are huge and happen in any year of transition to or from a situation where Test One becomes the condi-

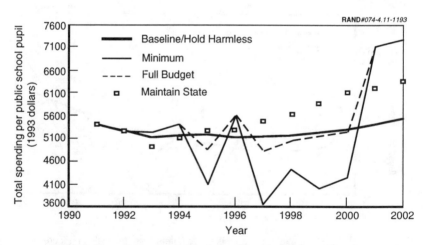

NOTE: The y-axis scale on this figure differs from the scale on Figures 4.2, 4.5, and 4.8. This reflects the wider variability associated with the shocks described in the analysis of this figure.

Figure 4.11—Total Spending Per Public School Pupil: No Double Hit, 34 Percent Shift

tion under which finances are calculated. Since they are unintentional and do not occur for several years, it is possible that the state will take action to mitigate these shifts before they occur. Absent additional action, however, these shifts are anticipated in a high-shift world.

Figure 4.11 shows the same shifts in the "Minimum" and "Full Budget" series in the 1996–97 and 2001–02 fiscal years, as the shifts between Test One and Test Two worlds act in conjunction with the no-double-hit assumption. The final policy space for the high-shift scenario is shown in Figure 4.12.

Comparing this figure to Figure 4.6, one can see that the result, on average, of the no-double-hit assumption under a high shift is to decrease the range of policy choices open to state decisionmakers. The minimum funding level under the double-hit assumption is an average of $18 billion, resulting in an average public per-pupil total of $4,300. In the no-double-hit interpretation, the minimum total state and local support to K–12 is more than $22.3 billion, while public schools receive nearly 20 percent more, or $5,111 per student.

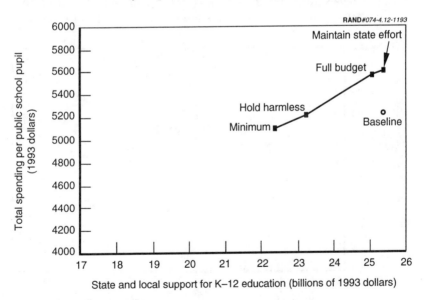

Figure 4.12—Policy Space: No Double Hit, 34 Percent Shift

SUMMARY

Figures 4.13 and 4.14 summarize the results of our analysis. Figure 4.13 represents the range of fiscal possibilities if the no-double-hit interpretation is the final word. Figure 4.14 represents the range of possibilities under a double-hit interpretation of the initiative.

In a no-double-hit world, if the shift is low, then the state will have to absorb the net higher cost of providing vouchers to students already in private schools in addition to its regular fiscal commitment to public schools. If the shift is large, then the state's discretion will expand. At a shift of somewhere around 15 to 20 percent, the voucher initiative will provide the state with a marginal fiscal benefit.

In the double-hit interpretation of Proposition 174, state policymakers have an increased measure of discretion in determining the level of K–12 finances. As Figure 4.14 shows, the state's fiscal options are spread out over a fairly wide range. In the double-hit scenario, the minimum funding level, represented in the figure by the lower-left endpoint of the line denoting the policy space, is always less than the baseline levels anticipated without vouchers, along both dimensions of interest—the total cost to the state of providing K–12 education

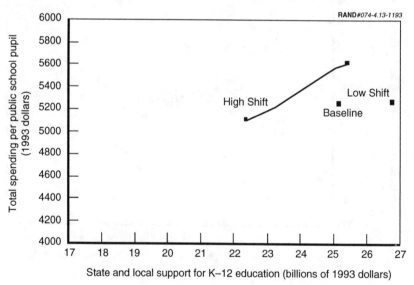

Figure 4.13—Policy Space: No Double Hit

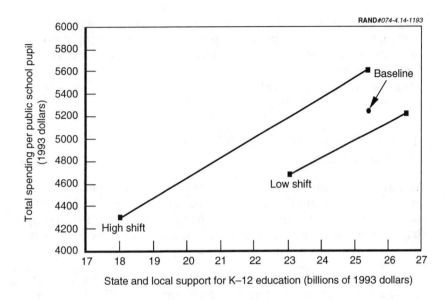

Figure 4.14—Policy Space: Double Hit

(state and local support of K–12 education) and the level of resources available, per pupil, to the public school system.

In both cases, the palatability of the eventual set of choices available to state policymakers will be framed in large part by the number of students who would have attended public schools absent vouchers, but chose to attend private schools under vouchers. A high shift will allow the state to choose between politically pleasant choices: reducing the total cost to the General Fund of providing K–12 education, increasing the level of investment in public K–12 education, or both. If the shift is small, the state will face politically unpleasant alternatives: increasing its General Fund support for K–12 education or cutting funds to public schools.

Another way of understanding this diagram is as follows. In the early years of the voucher system, the state inherits 550,000 students (originally in the private sector) for whom it must pay $2,600 each. This costs the state $1.4 billion. It can either pay this directly or, in a no-double-hit world, offset public education expenditures. As students leave the public system, however, it experiences savings because it has to pay only $2,600 for these students instead of $4,200.[5] At some level of shift, these savings produced by the shifting students offset the initial cost borne by the state for the private students, and the state begins to realize potential fiscal savings. As more students leave, additional savings will result, which the state can invest in either public K–12 or other activities.

SENSITIVITY OF OUR RESULTS TO THE INITIAL ASSUMPTIONS

We have based our analysis on projections of: (1) the likely demographic trends within the state's population, and specifically within the K–12 sector; (2) the future prospects of the state's economy, General Fund revenues, and property values; and (3) the level of inflation over the next decade.

To address this uncertainty, we have executed numerous iterations of this model, varying the levels of these inputs significantly. While these changes did change the actual numbers produced by our model, they did not affect the key result of our research—the definition of the relationships between the various policy alternatives and the baseline under the varying assumptions. The only exception was noted above, where changing to significantly lower economic estimates resulted in the disappearance of the first downward spike in Figure 4.10 in the no-double-hit, high-shift scenario. We are confident, then, that the relationships and the orders of magnitude discussed in this research are robust across the range of reasonable variations in the underlying inputs. For a detailed description of the results of the sensitivity analysis, see Appendix H.

------

[5]This $4,200 represents the current state and local property tax for K–12 students. The remaining $1,000 of the total $5,200 in resources comes from federal, lottery, and other local sources.

Chapter Five

CONCLUSIONS

The primary result of our analysis is simple: The fiscal effects of Proposition 174 are extremely uncertain. The initiative could save the state billions of dollars. Or it could cost the state more than a billion dollars a year. It could increase the resources available for each public school pupil by 7 percent. Or it could cut those resources by 18 percent. The bottom line is that no one knows. Thus, voting for Proposition 174 would be risky—but so would voting against it, since rising education costs are precipitating a state fiscal crisis.

Specifically:

1. Absent some intervention, the share of state General Fund revenues required to go to K–12 education over the next decade is expected to rise significantly, from 32 percent in 1993–94 to more than 43 percent in 2002–03. This increasing share is driven by expected high growth rates in the K–12 population, fueling a 38 percent increase over the next decade to nearly 8 million students in 2002–03.

2. Absent some intervention, the real level of per-pupil resources available to public schools will remain relatively flat over the next decade, growing at an annual average of only 0.5 percent. This growth rate reflects the fact that K–12 education finance in the state will be determined predominantly by Test Two of Proposition 98.

3. Implementation of the voucher initiative could significantly reduce K–12 education's demands on the state budget. Under a high-shift, double-hit scenario, the average required K–12 share

of the state General Fund over the next decade would decrease from 37 percent (without vouchers) to 20 percent, although this would also reduce total per-student resources available in public schools.

4. Implementation of the voucher initiative could significantly increase K–12 education's demands on the state budget. Under a low-shift, double-hit scenario, the state could be required to spend, on average, more than one billion extra dollars per year on K–12 education for the next decade without increasing resources to public schools at all.

5. Under most of the scenarios analyzed in this study, adopting Proposition 174 would reduce the Proposition 98-required minimum funding to public K–12 education. Not only does this hold in total terms, but also on a per-student basis. Under one scenario (a high-shift, double-hit interpretation), the minimum per-student commitment to public schools decreases by 18 percent. The net result of this finding is that if Proposition 174 passes, public K–12 education will be much more dependent on the generosity of the state to avoid such a large reduction.

6. The range of policy choices available to legislators will be defined by the number of students who choose to attend scholarship-redeeming schools instead of public schools. If this shift is high, then the state will be faced with favorable choices. If the shift is low, then the choices will be even more difficult than those that must be faced without a voucher system. Unfortunately, the size of the shift is unknown.

UNCERTAINTY IS THE KEY FINDING

With respect to the specific effects of the initiative on the public K–12 education's prospects, our research found a surprising diversity of results. The theme of our findings is uncertainty. The fiscal effects of the proposition could be strongly positive or strongly negative. The outcome depends on: (1) how certain provisions will govern the interaction of the initiative with Propositions 98 and 111; (2) the number of students who will shift from public schools to scholarship-redeeming schools; and (3) the spending policy that the state decides to pursue if vouchers are implemented. The available data are not sufficient to accurately predict the likely effects of Proposition 174 along any of these axes. Our research has looked at a variety of scenarios and alternatives across these three dimensions. The voters also must weigh the uncertainty across these dimensions and register their votes accordingly.

THE BOTTOM LINE

Four players in the game will in turn determine the fiscal effects of the voucher initiative on both the state's finances and K–12 education. The *voters* will play first on November 2, 1993, deciding whether the initiative will pass. If they vote no, the game is over. If they vote yes, then the *courts* will interpret the initiative with respect to the "double-hit" debate. The results of that decision will decide the policy space in which we operate. *Parents* will either shift their children to scholarship-redeeming schools or leave them in public schools. The aggregate level of these parents' decisions will define the range of subsequent policy choices available to the state. Finally, the *state* will take its turn by deciding how much it wishes to spend. The final result will be in either savings to the state budget—or additional costs; either more resources for public school pupils—or fewer resources. Until *all* four players have had their say, there is no way of knowing the ultimate effects of the voucher initiative.

One thing we do know, however: The state is facing a significant fiscal crisis—a crisis that will be exacerbated by the impending explosion in K–12 enrollments and its associated Proposition 98-driven demand for public resources. *Something* will have to change in the state's public finance system.

In sum, these findings represent a word of caution to *both* sides of the voucher debate. To those who believe that Proposition 174 is a good idea: The effects of the initiative could be fiscally detrimental to both the state and public K–12 education. To those who believe that the voucher initiative is a bad idea: A crisis is approaching in California's public finance system. The voucher initiative may help avoid an impossible fiscal situation.

A. DEMOGRAPHIC PROJECTIONS FOR CALIFORNIA

In our analysis, we used three population trends—the general population (for per-capita calculations), public K–12 enrollments, and private K–12 enrollments. This appendix presents the sources for these series as well as the assumptions related to their use. It provides the methodology used to develop and update the available series as well as the methodology for generating the high- and low-population series for the sensitivity analysis presented in Chapter Four and Appendix H.

POPULATION PROJECTIONS

The population projections used in this analysis were from the California Department of Finance's (DoF) Demographic Research Unit. They were produced in a specially requested run, using the most up-to-date revision (June 1993) of the DoF's projections for the state population through 2040. The values used are shown in Table A.1.

K–12 ENROLLMENT PROJECTIONS

The other key set of demographic series we used in our models was the public and private K–12 enrollments. For the purposes of our

Table A.1

California Population, 1991–92 to 2002–03

Year	Population (thousands)	Growth Rate (percent)
1991–92	30,646[a]	—
1992–93	31,300[a]	2.1
1993–94	31,906	1.9
1994–95	32,520	1.9
1995–96	33,188	2.1
1996–97	33,963	2.3
1997–98	34,524	1.7
1998–99	35,182	1.9
1999–00	35,824	1.8
2000–01	36,443	1.7
2001–02	37,044	1.6
2002–03	37,665	1.7

SOURCE: California Department of Finance, June 1993.

[a]Denotes actual values.

model, we have used the recent[1] Department of Finance projections of total K–12 public[2] and private[3] school enrollments (when available).   Because the public enrollment projections extend only through 2000–01, we developed estimates for 2001–02 and 2002–03. To derive the values for these years, we first adjusted the growth rates from the recent numbers by the rate of change in the growth rates from the June 1992 estimate. Equation (A.1) displays the mathematical derivation of the growth rates for 2001–02. A similar calculation was done for 2002–03, and the resulting growth rates were then applied to the recent enrollment estimate for 2000–01.

---

[1]The series were obtained in September 1993 and are from preliminary updates. These preliminary numbers are used because the most recent published series are from June 1991 (private enrollments) and June 1992 (public enrollments).

[2]The series, obtained from the Demographic Research Unit, is dated June 2, 1992, and represents the most recent series available at the time of this study.

[3]The series, obtained from the Demographic Research Unit, is dated June 18, 1991, and represents the most recent series available at the time of this study.

$$r \, {}^{\text{1993 estimate}}_{\text{2001-02}} = r \, {}^{\text{1993 estimate}}_{\text{2000-01}} \times \frac{r \, {}^{\text{1992 estimate}}_{\text{2001-02}}}{r \, {}^{\text{1992 estimate}}_{\text{2000-01}}} \quad\quad (A.1)$$

In the case of private enrollments, the most recent series available was the June 1991 series. We felt that there had been significant changes in the DoF estimates for public enrollments over that period, and since many of these changes were the result of broader demographic trends, they could affect private enrollments comparably. To reflect these changes, we adjusted the private enrollment growth rates from the 1991 series by the change between the new and old public enrollment series. This adjustment is presented in Equation (A.2).

$$r \, {}^{\text{1993 estimate}}_{\text{private}} = r \, {}^{\text{1991 estimate}}_{\text{private}} \times \frac{r \, {}^{\text{1993 estimate}}_{\text{public}}}{r \, {}^{\text{1992 estimate}}_{\text{public}}} \quad\quad (A.2)$$

These growth rates were then applied to the actual values from 1992–93 to generate the series below. The actual values used are presented in Table A.2.

Table A.2

Public and Private K–12 Enrollments, 1991–92 to 2002–03

Year	Public K–12 Enrollments (thousands)	Public K–12 Growth Rate (percent)	Private K–12 Enrollments (thousands)	Private K–12 Growth Rate (percent)
1991–92	5,002[a]	—	545[a]	—
1992–93	5,090[a]	1.8	554[a]	1.7
1993–94	5,172	1.6	556*	0.4
1994–95	5,294	2.4	561*	0.8
1995–96	5,456	3.1	571*	1.8
1996–97	5,656	3.7	582*	1.9
1997–98	5,871	3.8	593*	1.8
1998–99	6,094	3.8	605*	2.0
1999–00	6,321	3.7	616*	1.7
2000–01	6,553	3.7	626*	1.7
2001–02	6,782*	3.5	637*	1.7
2002–03	7,014*	3.4	648*	1.7

SOURCE: California Department of Finance projections, June 1991, 1992, and 1993.

(*) Denotes those derived from these series.

[a]Denotes actual values.

ADAs VERSUS HEADCOUNT ENROLLMENTS

One of the concerns of using these data series is that the state uses average daily attendance (ADA) in the various Proposition 98 tests, in compliance with the State Constitution and Education Code.[4]   While the Department of Finance produces estimates for public ADA attendance in K–12, these estimates project only through 1997–98 and do not include comparable projections for private enrollments. The former is problematic in that we wish to analyze through 2002–03 and the latter because the voucher initiative calls for the conversion between public and private enrollments for calculation purposes.[5]

We have chosen to use headcount enrollments for these two reasons. By using headcount enrollments, we are implicitly arguing that the conversion factor between headcounts and ADAs remains constant over time. In reviewing the ADA projections, it appears that there is some initial variability but that it generally levels out and remains constant. Since the K–12 finance tests generally are concerned with the changes in enrollments, and the relationship between headcounts and ADAs remains fairly constant, the use of headcounts does not significantly bias the results. To verify this effect, we analyzed our model using the ADA projections for the years they are available. The resulting series did not differ significantly from those presented in Chapter Four.

SENSITIVITY ADJUSTMENTS

Finally, we cannot account for all of the variations possible in the state's prospective demographics. For example, despite the ranges of series available, an unanticipated effect of the voucher initiative could be to increase interstate migration into California, as residents of other states migrate to California to take advantage of the voucher opportunity. If this occurred, it would increase both the state population and, more significant to this analysis, the K–12 demand on the state's resources. In the interests of parsimony, we have focused our

---

[4]See Sections 14022.3 and 14022.5 of the California Education Code.

[5]The voucher initiative calls for the allocation of vouchers on a per-student basis, raising the question of how the per-ADA mechanism of the Constitution and Education Code will be reconciled with this per-capita initiative.

analysis on the demographic scenarios estimated by the state and through our sensitivity mechanism.

To test the sensitivity of our analysis to the demographic projections presented in Tables A.1 and A.2, we have prepared a high and low estimate of each. To derive these series, we followed the Department of Finance's methodology for bounding its ADA projections. This approach assumes that the variance in the bounding series grows each year and is a function of the middle series. The general form for the high and low series is given by equations (A.3) and (A.4), respectively, where i is the number of years that year t is from year 1992–93 (e.g., for 1993–94: i = 1, 1994–95: i = 5, and so on).

$$\text{Series}_t^{\text{high}} = \left(\left[1 + 0.005 \left(t \right) \right] \right) \text{Series}_t^{\text{Middle}} \tag{A.3}$$

$$\text{Series}_t^{\text{low}} = \left(\left[1 - 0.005 \left(t \right) \right] \right) \text{Series}_t^{\text{Middle}} \tag{A.4}$$

See Table A.3 for the resulting high and low bounds for the three demographic inputs in our model.

Table A.3

Series Ranges for Demographic Variables

Year	Public K–12 Low Series	Public K–12 High Series	Private K–12 Low Series	Private K–12 High Series	Population Low Series	Population High Series
1991–92	5,002[a]	5,002[a]	545[a]	545[a]	30,646[a]	30,646[a]
1992–93	5,090[a]	5,090[a]	554[a]	554[a]	31,300[a]	31,300[a]
1993–94	5,148	5,200	554	559	31,761	32,079
1994–95	5,241	5,347	555	566	32,194	32,846
1995–96	5,374	5,538	563	580	32,691	33,685
1996–97	5,543	5,769	570	594	33,284	34,642
1997–98	5,724	6,018	578	608	33,661	35,387
1998–99	5,911	6,277	587	623	34,127	36,237
1999–00	6,100	6,542	594	637	34,570	37,078
2000–01	6,291	6,815	601	651	34,985	37,901
2001–02	6,477	7,087	608	665	35,377	38,711
2002–03	6,663	7,364	615	680	35,782	39,548

SOURCE: Derived from Department of Finance data using Equations (A.3) and (A.4).
[a]Denotes actual values.

B. MODELING THE CALIFORNIA ECONOMY

Calculation of the Proposition 98/111 guarantee and of the amount of the scholarship that would be provided under the voucher initiative requires the input of several economic and revenue variables. These variables include: General Fund revenues, personal income, local property taxes, lottery funds, federal funds, and other local revenues. For non-General Fund revenues to California, we are concerned with the share of those revenues that is allocated to K–12 education. These non-General Fund revenue sources are addressed in Appendix C. Both the economic and revenue numbers were projected to the year 2002–03 to provide a ten-year analysis of the voucher initiative.

This appendix provides a description of our efforts at modeling General Fund revenues and personal income. In addition, as these numbers are highly uncertain, sensitivity analyses were performed on them. The projections used in the sensitivity analyses are also discussed here.

GENERAL FUND REVENUE FORECAST

The General Fund revenue numbers through 1991–92 are historical actuals. Beginning in 1992–93 through 1994–95, the numbers are projections from the Commission on State Finance reported in the June 1993 *Quarterly General Fund Forecast.* The General Fund forecast of the Commission on State Finance is lower than that of the Governor's Budget by $27 million in 1992–93, $711 million in 1993–94, and $766 million in 1994–95. The difference between the two forecasts is due primarily to different assumptions about the growth in personal income taxes. About 90 percent of General Fund revenues come from three sources—personal income taxes (42 percent), sales taxes (37 percent), and bank and corporation taxes (11 percent). The Commission on State Finance is assuming that much of the current 1992–93 gain in personal income taxes is due to one-time factors, while the Administration is assuming that the gains seen in the current year will continue.

Our research could not find any current forecast of California General Fund revenues or personal income beyond 1994–95. Long-term forecasts had been produced by the Commission on State Finance through 1991, but these were based upon sustained growth throughout the decade and did not include the deep recession that hit the state in the early 1990s. Therefore, for 1995–96 through 2002–03, we relied on our own forecasts. We deliberately kept the assumptions behind the forecasts simple and relied on sensitivity analyses to determine how our results would or would not change as we varied the economic assumptions. Our base forecast for General Fund revenues is shown in Table B.1. General Fund revenues growth rates were based on historical growth rates, discussions with the Commission on State Finance, and sensitivity for the historical relationship between the growth of General Fund revenues and other economic variables.

California General Fund revenues grew on average by about 8.5 percent in nonrecessionary years in the 1980s. Actual and projected growth rates for the early to mid-1990s are well below this average. The exception to this was a growth rate of 10 percent in 1991–92. This relatively strong positive growth rate was in large part due to a number of temporary revenue-enhancing provisions passed with the 1991 Budget Act. The bulk of the increase in revenues is related to higher sales tax rates, an extension of the sales tax to candy and snack foods and other items, increases in the marginal personal income tax rates on high-income taxpayers, and a two-year suspension of net operating loss carryforward deductions for corporations. The 1991 Budget Act also put major taxes on an accrual basis for a one-time gain of about $1.4 billion in 1991–92. The revenues gained from these provisions continue to diminish over time because most of the measures were temporary.

Table B.1

Economic Trends, Base Case: California's General Fund and
Personal Income

	General Fund		Personal Income	
Year	$billions	% growth	$billions	% growth
1986–87	32.5	15.8	453.4	7.4
1987–88	32.5	0.0	491.4	8.4
1988–89	37.0	13.6	531.0	8.1
1989–90	38.7	4.9	576.5	8.6
1990–91	38.2	–1.4	616.7	7.0
1991–92	42.0	10.0	624.0	1.2
1992–93	41.0	–2.5	641.4	2.8
1993–94	39.5	–3.7	665.6	3.8
1994–95	41.5	5.2	697.1	4.7
1995–96	43.6	5.0	733.4	5.2
1996–97	44.8	2.7	770.1	5.0
1997–98	47.0	5.0	808.6	5.0
1998–99	49.4	5.0	849.0	5.0
1999–00	52.3	6.0	899.9	6.0
2000–01	55.5	6.0	953.9	6.0
2001–02	59.4	7.0	1020.7	7.0
2002–03	63.5	7.0	1092.2	7.0

SOURCE: Through 1994–95 the numbers are from the Commission on State
Finance, *Quarterly General Fund Forecast* (various years).

In contrast to 1991–92, the growth in General Fund revenues for
1990–91 was –1.4 percent, and the projected growth rates by both the
Commission on State Finance and the Administration for 1992–93
and 1993–94 are negative. A turnaround in the negative growth rates
is projected for 1994–95. The Commission on State Finance estimates that General Fund revenues will grow by 5.2 percent in 1994.
Our base forecast assumes that General Fund revenues will continue
on a path of positive growth, working toward their prerecessionary
average growth rates. Clearly, there is a great deal of uncertainty
about future economic growth in California. Our base case assumes
that we see some recovery in growth rates beginning in 1994–95 and
that California continues a slow recovery toward 1980 nonrecessionary growth rates in General Fund revenues throughout the mid- to
late 1990s and into the early 2000s.

An exception to this occurs in 1996–97. We project growth in General Fund revenues to slow to 2.7 percent in 1996–97 because of the expiration of the 1991 law that put into effect higher marginal personal income tax rates on high-income taxpayers. Based on conversations with the Commission on State Finance, we estimate that the elimination of that provision will lower General Fund revenues by about $1 billion a year. There are other provisions in law that will expire over the projection period, but their expected effect on General Fund revenues is small.

PERSONAL INCOME FORECAST

The personal income numbers through 1991–92 in Table B.1 are historical actuals. Beginning in 1992–93 through 1994–95, the numbers are projections from the Commission on State Finance's June 1993 *Quarterly General Fund Forecast*. The 1996–97 through 2002–03 projections are our own based on historical growth rates, discussions with the Commission on State Finance, and sensitivity for the historical relationship between the growth of General Fund revenues and personal income.

Personal income and General Fund revenues have historically had almost unitary growth. Adjusting for legislative changes that have affected General Fund revenues, we find General Fund revenues have grown roughly in line with personal income. Therefore, in years in which there are no legislative changes that cause the growth rates of the two variables to diverge, we would expect to see similar growth rates of the two economic variables. The growth rate of personal income historically has been about 95 percent of the growth rate of General Fund revenues.

Making no assumptions about future legislative action, we assume that the growth rates of General Fund revenues and personal income will be similar from 1997–98 to 2002–03. Clearly, this is a simplifying assumption because there have been temporary changes in tax laws throughout the late 1980s and early 1990s that have caused the two economic variables to diverge. The one exception to our assumption that General Fund revenues and personal income will grow at similar rates is in 1996–97. Once again, this is because of the expiration of the temporary increase in the marginal personal income tax rate on high-income taxpayers that was put into effect in 1991. We assume that this change will affect General Fund revenue growth but not personal income growth.

As seen in Table B.1, personal income grew quite consistently between about 7.5 and 8.5 percent in nonrecessionary years in the 1980s. The projections for personal income for 1993–94 and 1994–95 from the Commission on State Finance assume that growth in personal income will begin to pick up from the unusually low rates of growth in the early 1990s. As with General Fund revenues, our base forecast for 1996 through 2002 for personal income assumes that growth in personal income gradually returns to its prerecessionary averages.

SENSITIVITY ANALYSES

As both General Fund revenues and personal income are prominent in the calculation of the Proposition 98/111 guarantee and are highly uncertain variables, we performed some sensitivity analyses on them. Tables B.2 and B.3 present a series of relatively optimistic and relatively pessimistic assumptions regarding General Fund revenues and personal income.

The optimistic forecast for General Fund revenues is based on the *Annual Long-Term General Fund Forecast, Fall 1990* from the Commission on State Finance. The growth rates for General Fund revenues for 1993–94 through 2002–03 are taken from that report. The report was done before the recession had hit California, and, therefore, the rates of growth are similar to those seen in the nonrecessionary years of the 1980s. The report projects General Fund revenues only out to 2000–01, and so we assumed the same rate of growth for 2001–02 and 2002–03 that is predicted for 2000–01. This set of growth rates suggests a scenario in which, beginning in 1993–94, California rapidly moves out of the current recession and growth in General Fund revenues remains strong over the projection period.

As in the base case assumptions, the optimistic scenarios in Tables B.2 and B.3 assume that personal income and General Fund revenues grow at the same rate. Again, the only year for which the rates of growth differ is 1996–97 because of the change in the tax law that we estimate will lower General Fund revenues by about $1 billion a year.

Table B.2

Economic Trends, Optimistic and Pessimistic Scenarios: California's General Fund

	Optimistic		Pessimistic	
Year	$billions	% growth	$billions	% growth
1993–94	43.8	6.8	38.9	−5.0
1994–95	47.0	7.3	40.4	3.7
1995–96	50.6	7.8	41.7	3.2
1996–97	53.6	5.8	42.2	1.3
1997–98	57.9	8.0	43.5	3.1
1998–99	62.6	8.1	44.9	3.1
1999–00	67.8	8.3	46.8	4.3
2000–01	73.5	8.5	48.8	4.2
2001–02	79.8	8.5	51.6	5.8
2002–03	86.6	8.5	54.6	5.8

Table B.3

Economic Trends, Optimistic and Pessimistic Scenarios: California's Personal Income

	Optimistic		Pessimistic	
Year	$billions	% growth	$billions	% growth
1993–94	685.0	6.8	647.8	1.0
1994–95	735.0	7.3	672.0	3.7
1995–96	792.4	7.8	693.6	3.2
1996–97	854.2	7.8	715.7	3.2
1997–98	922.5	8.0	738.1	3.1
1998–99	997.2	8.1	760.9	3.1
1999–00	1080.0	8.3	793.9	4.3
2000–01	1171.8	8.5	827.5	4.2
2001–02	1271.4	8.5	875.2	5.8
2002–03	1379.5	8.5	925.7	5.8

For the pessimistic scenarios, we took the difference in growth rates between the base case scenario and the optimistic scenario and re-versed that growth. For example, in 1995–96, the growth in General Fund revenues is estimated to be 5 percent in the base case scenario. In the optimistic scenario, the growth rate is estimated at 7.8 percent. The difference in the growth rates between the two is 0.56, or $(7.8/5.0) - 1$. Then we took $5.0/(1 + 0.56)$ to calculate the pessimistic scenario rate of growth for General Fund revenues for 1995–96 of 3.2 percent.

This same calculation was used to get from the optimistic to the pessimistic scenario in every year except for 1993–94. In 1993–94, because we are estimating negative growth for General Fund revenues in our base case scenario, this calculation would have produced an unusually low rate of growth for General Fund revenues under the pessimistic scenario. We assume in 1993–94 under the optimistic scenario that General Fund revenues will grow 6.8 percent. This is considerably higher than the base case of –3.7 percent growth. If we reversed that rate of growth for the pessimistic scenario, we would get negative growth of about 14 percent in General Fund revenues in 1993–94. Such a negative rate of growth in General Fund revenues has not been experienced even in the worst recessionary years. Therefore, we assumed a negative growth rate of 5 percent in 1993–94, which is about double that expected to be seen in 1992–93.

The pessimistic scenario assumes that the current recession continues to get worse for another year and then a slow and moderate recovery begins. It is assumed that the recovery does not return California to rates of growth in General Fund revenues or personal income that were experienced in nonrecessionary years in the 1980s. While the average growth rate in the pessimistic personal income series of 3.7 percent may not seem that pessimistic, it is important to remember that this is (1) *total* personal income, (2) occurring during a period of high population growth, and (3) stated in nominal terms. Per-capita personal income, under this pessimistic scenario, would grow at only 2.2 percent a year in nominal terms—a rate likely slower than inflation itself.

C. PROJECTING NONSTATE SOURCES OF K–12 FUNDS

There are several sources of revenue to California's K–12 education sector besides those from the General Fund. These include local property taxes, lottery funds, federal funds, and other local funds. All of these funds are used in the calculation of the amount of the scholarship that would be available under the voucher initiative, and local property taxes are used in the calculation of the Proposition 98/111 guarantee. The revenue numbers were projected to the year 2002–03 to provide a ten-year analysis of the voucher initiative. This appendix will provide a description of our efforts at projecting these sources of revenue to 2002–03, including the calculations and the assumptions behind the projections. Sensitivity analyses were performed on the local property tax projections as these numbers are prominent in the calculation of the Proposition 98/111 guarantee. All numbers reported in this appendix are allocations to K–12 education only.

An important note to make is that we have made no assumptions about how these various sources of revenue to K–12 education would change if students switched from public schools to private schools under a voucher program. It is very possible that some part of these revenues to public K–12 education would in fact go away if fewer students were enrolled in K–12 public education.

LOCAL PROPERTY TAX FORECAST

The local property taxes allocated to K–12 education for 1986–87 through 1991–92 are historical actuals. Local property taxes allocated to K–12 education grew at about 8 percent a year throughout the 1980s. Growth in the early 1990s kept pace with this average, reaching 9.5 percent in 1990–91 and 7.2 percent in 1991–92. This is in sharp contrast to what appears will be the rate of growth in local property taxes allocated to K–12 education for 1992–93. The Governor's 1992–93 Budget shifted $1.3 billion in local revenues from local governments (cities, counties, special districts, redevelopment agencies, and enterprise districts) to K–12 school districts and community college districts. Almost the entirety of these additional local revenues went to K–12 school districts. The result is that local property tax revenues allocated to K–12 education are expected to grow by about 19.5 percent between 1991–92 and 1992–93. Without this shift, local revenues to K–12 education would have actually fallen by about 3 percent, largely reflecting current recessionary pressures. The additional property tax revenues do not increase the resources available to K–12 education but rather reduce the burden on state General Fund revenues. The local property tax shift results in a larger share of total resources to K–12 education being provided by local property taxes.

The projections for the local property taxes allocated to K–12 education, as well as other miscellaneous sources of income to K–12 education, are shown in Table C.1.

The estimated large growth rate of close to 35 percent in local revenues to K–12 education between 1992–93 and 1993–94, from $6.73 billion to $9.01 billion, is again due to a shift in local property taxes. The 1993–94 Governor's Budget calls for a $2.6 billion permanent shift in local revenues from local governments to K–12 school districts and community colleges. Again, the shift would not result in a net increase in funding for K–12 education, but rather would result in an equivalent $2.6 billion reduction in General Fund outlays. Counties and special districts are expected to bear the majority of the property tax shift, with cities and redevelopment agencies facing a smaller reduction.

Our forecast for 1992–93 through 2002–03 does not assume any additional shifts in local property tax revenues. There is still about an additional $7 billion in local property taxes that, in the future, could be allocated to K–12 education. Our base forecast for local property taxes to K–12 education assumes a growth rate of about 2.5 percent

Table C.1

Non-General Fund Sources of Revenue for K–12 Education
(in $billions)

Year	Local Property Taxes	Lottery Funds	Federal Funds	Other Local Funds
1986–87	3.80	.41	1.17	.98
1987–88	4.11	.59	1.35	1.59
1988–89	4.47	.91	1.52	1.77
1989–90	4.80	.78	1.63	1.94
1990–91	5.25	.60	1.77	1.77
1991–92	5.63	.40	2.01	1.77
1992–93	6.73	.56	2.24	1.93
1993–94	9.01	.56	2.23	2.10
1994–95	9.23	.59	2.43	2.29
1995–96	9.50	.64	2.65	2.50
1996–97	9.84	.69	2.88	2.72
1997–98	10.28	.74	3.14	2.97
1998–99	10.74	.78	3.43	3.24
1999–00	11.31	.85	3.73	3.53
2000–01	11.92	.91	4.07	3.84
2001–02	12.57	.98	4.44	4.19
2002–03	13.37	1.07	4.84	4.57

SOURCE: 1986–87 through 1991–92 figures are from the *Analysis of the 1993–94 Budget Bill*, Office of the Legislative Analyst, State of California.

in 1994–95, increasing to about 6 percent by 2002–03. These growth rates appear low compared with historical average growth rates of nearly 8 percent because we have assumed that the $2.6 billion property tax shift that will go into effect in 1993–94 is not adjusted for inflation. Therefore, the permanent shift of $2.6 billion in nominal dollars results in overall rates of growth in total property taxes allocated to K–12 education being considerably lower than historical averages.

Excluding the $2.6 billion shift, we assume that local property tax collections for K–12 education grow in line with our base case assumptions as outlined in Appendix B. Our base case forecast assumes that we see some recovery in growth rates beginning in 1994–95, and that California continues a slow recovery toward 1980 nonrecessionary growth rates throughout the mid- to late 1990s and into the early 2000s. Removing the $2.6 billion shift in each year from

1993–94 through 2002–03 from the local property tax figures in Table C.1 results in a growth rate of about 3.5 percent in 1995–96, increasing steadily to about 8 percent by 2002–03.

Because local property taxes figure into the calculation of the Proposition 98/111 guarantee, we have performed some sensitivity calculations around them. Table C.2 below presents the optimistic and pessimistic property tax scenarios used in our sensitivity analysis.

As in the optimistic scenarios for General Fund revenues and personal income described in Appendix B, the optimistic scenario for local property taxes assumes a set of growth rates in which California moves out of the current recession quite rapidly and the growth in local property taxes remains strong over the projection period. As stated above for the base case scenario, the growth rates under the optimistic scenario look unusually low because we assume that the $2.6 billion permanent shift in local revenues beginning in 1993–94 is not adjusted for inflation. Taking the $2.6 billion out of the above figures in each year would result in growth rates of about 8.5 percent beginning in 1997–98. This is slightly above the average growth rate of local property taxes allocated to K–12 education in the 1980s.

As explained in Appendix B, for the pessimistic scenarios we took the difference in the growth rates between the base case scenario and

Table C.2

Economic Trends, Optimistic and Pessimistic Scenarios: Local Property Taxes, K–12 Education

Year	Optimistic		Pessimistic	
	$billions	% growth	$billions	% growth
1993–94	9.01	33.8	9.01	33.8
1994–95	9.23	2.5	9.23	2.5
1995–96	9.67	4.7	9.40	1.8
1996–97	10.20	5.5	9.62	2.4
1997–98	10.84	6.3	9.92	3.1
1998–99	11.54	6.5	10.23	3.1
1999–00	12.30	6.6	10.67	4.3
2000–01	13.13	6.7	11.14	4.4
2001–02	14.02	6.8	11.63	4.4
2002–03	14.99	6.9	12.31	5.8

the optimistic scenario and reversed that growth. For example, in 1995–96, the growth in local property taxes excluding the $2.6 billion shift is estimated to be 4.0 percent in the base case scenario. In the optimistic scenario, the growth rate is estimated at 6.5 percent. The difference in the growth rates between the two is 0.62, or (6.5 ÷ 4.0) − 1. Then, we took 4.0 ÷ (1 + 0.62) to calculate the pessimistic scenario rate of growth for local property taxes excluding the $2.6 billion shift for 1995–96 of 2.5 percent. The pessimistic scenario assumes that California faces a slow and moderate recovery. It also assumes that California does not return to prerecessionary rates of growth by 2002–03.

LOTTERY FUNDS AND OTHER LOCAL FUNDS

Lottery funds have been allocated to K–12 education since 1985. The 1986–87 through 1991–92 figures in Table C.1 are historical actuals, the 1992–93 and 1993–94 figures are from the 1993–94 Governor's Budget, and the 1994–95 through 2002–03 figures are our own estimates. Lottery fund revenues have tended to follow economic trends, particularly trends in personal income. Lottery fund revenues grew rapidly in the mid- to late 1980s before experiencing negative growth in the early 1990s. We grew lottery funds over the projection period under the assumption that they will continue to follow economic trends. In addition, we assumed that their allocation to K–12 education is dependent upon K–12 school enrollment. Therefore, we grew lottery funds allocated to K–12 education each year in proportion to the product of K–12 school enrollments and per-capita personal income. This resulted in growth rates that averaged about 7.3 percent from 1994–95 to 2000–01 and about 8 percent in the 2000s.

Other local funds include a wide variety of local support. Included in this category are things such as: building funds, sale of property, sale of bonds, cafeteria funds, and food services sales. A complete listing of other local funds is included in *Financial Transactions of School Districts* from the Office of the Controller. Other local revenues from 1992–93 through 2002–03 in Table C.1 are our own estimates, the other years being historical actuals. Since other local revenues historically have grown by about 9 percent a year, we have assumed that rate of growth for each year from 1992–93 through 2002–03.

FEDERAL FUNDS

The federal government provides funding for a variety of programs that support K–12 education. It is particularly important to note here that we are assuming in the figures that appear in Table C.1 that federal support continues to grow at historical rates. As some federal support is determined per student in the public sector, it is likely that as students switch to the private sector under a voucher program, some of this federal money will no longer be available to public K–12 education. For this reason, we list the federal money allocated to K–12 education in Table C.3 below and include some description of the funding.

Numbers in Table C.1 for federal funds for 1986–87 through 1991–92 are historical actuals, for 1992–93 through 1994–95 are projections from the Governor's 1993–94 Budget, and for 1995–96 through 2002–03 are our own projections. Federal funds to California's K–12 education historically have grown at about 9 percent a year. Virtually all of this money goes to public K–12 education. We assumed for our projections that federal funds allocated to K–12 education continue to grow at 9 percent a year.

It is unclear how federal funding for California's K–12 education would change under a voucher program. Table C.3 shows some numbers and descriptions to provide information on which federal

Table C.3

1992–93 Federal K–12 Education Funding in California

Program	$millions
Child Nutrition	860
Chapter 1	560
Special Education	230
Migrant Education	106
Vocational Education	101
Child Care	74
Chapter 2	42
Drug-Free Schools	42
Total	2,015

SOURCE: California Department of Education.

programs fund California's K–12 education. We have included only programs that provide at least $25 million to California's K–12 education.

Child Nutrition is a federal school breakfast and lunch program for students of low-income families. The federal money is allocated per meal served, not per student served, in public schools. If a low-income student who received school lunch transferred to a private school and no new student at the public school received a free lunch in the student's place, then the federal money for California's K–12 education could be reduced.

Chapter 1 provides supplemental and remedial services to students who are at least two years behind in the curriculum. The money is directed to the public schools based on the income of the student's family. This is a per-pupil calculation and so may affect public school revenues if particular students switched to private schools. But the calculations involved in providing the benefits are so complicated that the results for California's public schools would be difficult to determine.

The federal Special Education program currently provides funding primarily to public schools. The state provides about $9 for every $1 of federal funding for special education. A small portion of this funding now goes to private education when it is determined that the public school cannot deliver the required services.

Migrant education is delivered through regional offices, and its funding is unlikely to be affected by a voucher program. Child Care, Chapter 2, and Drug Free Schools programs are also unlikely to be affected by vouchers. Vocational Education is funded through a variety of formula grants that provide funds to states and localities in support of vocational education programs and to promote equal opportunity in vocational programs for historically underserved populations. It is unclear how federal funds allocated to public schools would be affected if students were to switch to the private sector.

D. CALIFORNIA'S EDUCATION FINANCE: MODELING PROPOSITIONS 98 AND 111

The first major task in our simulation of the effects of the voucher on K–12 finance is to model the provisions of the California Constitution and Education Code, which are defined by Propositions 98 and 111. Proposition 98 provides a minimum floor for the funding levels of K–14 education.

Conceptually, Proposition 98 creates a *baseline* level of funding for K–14 education in California. The state education spending floor remains on this baseline, which is defined by Tests 1 and 2 of the State Constitution, Section 8, subdivision (b), unless it encounters economic hard times.

When the state encounters bad times, however, Test 3 of the same section takes over and allows the state to spend less than the baseline amounts. When this happens, the shortfall between what is actually spent and the baseline is called the *maintenance factor*. When the bad times pass, provisions kick in that cause the state to return to the baseline and, in effect, repay the maintenance factor. This process is called *restoration.*

As we turn now to describing the formal model, it is important to consider that the central focus of this analysis is the effect of the voucher initiative on K–12 finance. Accordingly, we have chosen not to include community college finances in our analysis. To exclude the community college portion from the Test 1, 2, and 3 calculations of the Proposition 98 guarantee amounts, we have allocated 90 percent of the Proposition 98 money to K–12 and the balance to community colleges. Historically, the split between K–12 and community colleges has been around 90–10, and absent any choices by the state to act otherwise, it will presumably remain so over the balance of this decade. The specific details regarding the implementation of this assumption in our model will be presented below.

VARIABLES AND CONVENTIONS

We will be presenting the mathematical forms of our model and its underlying equations in the course of this appendix. To facilitate understanding, we will use the following variables throughout the appendix. All terms are nominal for the purposes of executing the simulation model. Results are subsequently deflated by the appropriate inflation rate for reporting in this analysis.

t: This is an index for the given year.

α: This coefficient represents the required minimum proportion of the state's General Fund revenues that must go to K–12 education under Proposition 98 under Test 1.

$A1_t$: This is the Test 1 calculated amount used for calculating the actual Proposition 98 minimum funding guarantee.

$A2_t$: This is the Test 2 calculated amount used for calculating the actual Proposition 98 minimum funding guarantee.

$A3_t$: This is the Test 3 calculated amount used for calculating the actual Proposition 98 minimum funding guarantee.

$A3a_t$: This is the Test 3a calculated amount used for calculating the actual Proposition 98 minimum funding guarantee.

$A3b_t$: This is the Test 3b calculated amount used for calculating the actual Proposition 98 minimum funding guarantee.

B_t: The state and local commitment to education in year t. It equals the K–12 portion of the state General Fund and those local property taxes allocated for K–12 education.

E_t: Total K–12 headcount enrollment in public schools in year t.

G_t: The state General Fund in year t.

H_t: The per-capita state General Fund in year t, arrived at by dividing G_t by P_t.

I_t: Total personal income in California in year t.

J_t: Per-capita state personal income in year t, derived by dividing I_t by P_t.

N_t: The "hypothetical baseline" in year t. The hypothetical baseline is a value used in calculating the restoration of the maintenance factor in post-Test 3 (see below) or post-suspension years.[1] It is equal to the level of the minimum funding guarantee in year t if the suspension or Test 3 had never occurred in a prior year.

$N1_t$: This is the Test 1 calculated amount used for calculating the baseline.

$N2_t$: This is the Test 2 calculated amount used for calculating the baseline.

$N3_t$: This is the cap by which the Test 2 baseline amount is allowed to grow after a Test 1 year.

P_t: The state population in year t.

R_t: The amount of the maintenance factor to be restored in a year t (see below for discussion of restoration of maintenance factors).

S_t: The state General Fund budget for K–12 education in year t, also equal to $(B_t - X_t)$.

X_t: The portion of local property taxes allocated to K–12 education in year t.

In addition, we will present the calculations to derive the Proposition 98/111 guarantee amount associated with each of the three tests. We

----

[1] The state has the option of suspending the Proposition 98 funding requirements in a given year.

will call the result of the Test 1 calculation A1, A2 for Test 2, A3a for Test 3a, and A3b for Test 3b.

The first stage in our analysis is to calculate the baseline floor for K–12 spending. We will use two terms with similar but very specific meanings in this appendix—baselines and budgets. The baseline represents the hypothetical level of spending that would occur for K–12 absent any interruptions due to poor economic years and suspensions.[2] The budget represents the *actual* spending in a given year. If a Test 3 year never occurs, then the two are equal.

With these conventions in hand, the analysis can now turn to modeling K–12 finance in California.

THE BASELINE

The first step in our analysis is to calculate the baseline amounts for K–12 education over the next decade. In spirit, this baseline is what the education budget would have been if the General Fund had grown enough to support the "Test 1–Test 2" amounts. The specific language guiding the calculations for the baseline amounts for Tests 1 and 2 is provided in California Constitution Article XVI, Section 8, subdivision (b), paragraphs (1) and (2), respectively.[3] The baseline amount in any year is given by the greater of Test 1 and 2 amounts as they are specified in Section 8. Let us now detail these two amounts.

Test 1

Test 1 requires that a minimum proportion of the California General Fund be allocated to K–12 education. The total[4] baseline amount allocated to K–12 education under this scenario is then given in Equation (D.1).

---

[2]Most of the provisions of Proposition 98 can be suspended for one year. This analysis does not consider the effects of suspensions of these provisions.

[3]We have provided the excerpts from the California Constitution and the California Education Code for all of the cited sections in Appendix G.

[4]In this appendix, as in the analysis in this report, the state commitment to K–12 is defined as the total state General Fund commitment plus total local property tax proceeds allocated to K–12 education. The explanation for this as a unit of analysis is included in the introduction to Chapter Four.

$$Nl_t = \alpha G_t + X_t \tag{D.1}$$

For K–14 education the share of the General Fund was 40.7 percent in 1991–92, 37.7 percent in 1992–93, and 33.1 percent in 1993–94. The changes are the result of adjusting to the increased use of local property taxes to fund education. In order to convert these parameters to K–12 dollars only, we have multiplied them by 90 percent.[5] Multiplying the shares above and converting them to decimals yield the following values for α, the multiplier in Equation (D.1): 0.367 for 1991–92, 0.339 for 1992–93, and 0.297 for 1993–94 and subsequent years.

Test 2

The Test 2 amount is defined by the language in Article XVI, Section (8)(b)(2). It requires that real per-pupil expenditures this year at least equal the prior year's expenditures. Equation (D.2) presents that calculation.

$$N2_t = N_{t-1}\left(\frac{E_t}{E_{t-1}}\right)\left(\frac{J_t}{J_{t-1}}\right) \tag{D.2}$$

Note that, in general, this year's Test 2 amount is a function of last year's baseline amount (N_{t-1}), not the prior year's baseline Test 2 amount, $N2_{t-1}$. If, in the prior year, N_t was determined by Test 1 (N1 > N2) and Test 1 represented extraordinary growth levels, then the potential would exist for a significant "ratcheting up" of the baseline amount. The state took this into account in implementing Proposition 98 and included a 1.5 percent growth cap on Test 1 in a given year.[6] We implement this cap in Equation (D.3).[7]

$$N3_t = \left(0.015\right)G_{t-1} \tag{D.3}$$

---

[5]Historically, K–12 has received approximately 90 percent of the total Proposition 98 guarantee amount. We assume that this share will continue into the future.

[6]See subdivision (c) of Section 8, Article XVI, of the California Constitution.

[7]Remember that this calculation is for the hypothetical baseline amount. The actual Proposition 98 guarantee in a year can exceed this cap because of Test 1.

Putting these all together, we arrive at Equation (D.4) for the final determination of the baseline amount. This equation says that the hypothetical baseline amount in year t equals at least the Test 2 amount plus some other amounts. If Test 1 is greater than Test 2, the equation adds either the difference between the Test 1 and Test 2 amount (resulting in the full Test 1 amount) or the 1.5 percent cap on baseline growth, whichever is smaller. If Test 1 is smaller than Test 2, then it adds zero to the Test 2 total, resulting in the Test 2 amount.

$$N_t = N2 + \min\left\{\max\left[\left(N1_t - N2_t\right), 0\right], N3_t\right\} \qquad (D.4)$$

It is important to remember that this baseline amount is the hypothetical amount that K–12 education would receive in a world where the General Fund always grows faster than inflation. Let us now turn to the actual amounts guaranteed to K–12 education.

THE BUDGET FOR K–12 EDUCATION

The next step in modeling K–12 finance, determining the budget for K–12 education, follows a methodology similar in many respects to that of the baseline. The difference is that it also allows for low-growth years through the introduction of Test 3 calculations. In a given year, one of the three tests specified in Section 8, subdivision (b), will apply. We will now step briefly through each of these tests and then finish with an analysis of how they interrelate and when they apply within a given year.

The Test 1 Amount

The budget may be represented by a linear function of the General Fund as in the Test 1 calculation above. Equation (D.5) shows the linear relationship between the General Fund and the Test 1 budget amount.

$$A1_t = aG_t + X_t \qquad (D.5)$$

The Test 2 Amount

Similarly, the Test 2 budget might be last year's budget increased by enrollment growth[8] and inflation (per-capita personal income) growth (the Test 2 amount):

$$A2_t = B_{t-1} \left(\frac{E_t}{E_{t-1}} \right) \left(\frac{J_t}{J_{t-1}} \right) \tag{D.6}$$

It is important to point out that B_{t-1}, last year's state and local spending on K–12 education, in this equation represents the prior year's actual spending—the budget—and not the baseline. In periods of state economic prosperity, $A2_t$ is subject to the same growth constraints as $N2_t$ and therefore B_{t-1} cannot exceed N_{t-1}.

The Test 3 Amount

In low General Fund revenue growth years, the budget is determined by Test 3. Under one provision of this test, the budget is last year's budget increased by enrollment growth and General Fund (per-capita) growth plus one-half of 1 percent (the "Test 3a" amount), as described in Section (8)(b)(3).[9] We have given it mathematically in Equation (D.7). Note that B_{t-1} in the equations in this section represents the actual spending, the budget, from the prior year.

$$A3a_t = B_{t-1} \left(\frac{E_t}{E_{t-1}} \right) \left[\left(\frac{H_t}{H_{t-1}} \right) + 0.005 \right] \tag{D.7}$$

Test 3, however, is further constrained by Section 41203.5 of the Education Code, which requires that K–14 education, on a per-pupil basis, do no worse than noneducation categories within the General

---

[8]There is a constraint that, in years of declining enrollment, the enrollment adjustment cannot serve to reduce the funding amount *unless* there were also enrollment decreases in the prior **two** years. This applies in both Tests 2 and 3a.

[9]See Appendix G for the full text of this section of the California Constitution.

Fund, on a per-capita basis.[10] This is "Test 3b." Another way of stating this is that this year's budget might be last year's budget increased by enrollment growth and the growth in noneducation spending from the General Fund. This is given in Equation (D.8).

$$A3b_t = B_{t-1}\left(\frac{E_t}{E_{t-1}}\right)\left(\frac{(G_t - S_t)/P_t}{(G_{t-1} - S_{t-1})/P_{t-1}}\right) \tag{D.8}$$

Recognizing that $S_t = B_t - X_t$ and $S_{t-1} = B_{t-1} - X_{t-1}$ in general, and that $B_t = A3b_t$ in this formula, one can solve for $A3b_t$, defining an intermediate variable, Z_t, to make the final formula more compact. We have done this in equations (D.9) and (D.10) below. We will limit explanation to the fact that they represent the algebraic solutions of Equation (D.8), solving for $A3b_t$.

$$Z_t = \left(\frac{P_{t-1}}{P_t}\right)\left(\frac{1}{G_{t-1} - B_{t-1} + X_{t-1}}\right) \tag{D.9}$$

$$A3b_t = \frac{B_{t-1}\left(\dfrac{E_t}{E_{t-1}}\right)Z_t(G_t + X_t)}{1 + Z_t B_{t-1}\left(\dfrac{E_t}{E_{t-1}}\right)} \tag{D.10}$$

The final Test 3 amount is equal to the greater of $A3a_t$ or $A3b_t$, as long as it does not exceed $A2_t$. In equation form, one gets Equation (D.11).

$$A3_t = \min\left[\max(A3a_t, A3b_t), A2_t\right] \tag{D.11}$$

Moreover, if one is in a Test 3 world, then the budget is below the baseline. The difference between the two is called the maintenance factor. Since our model keeps the baseline from year-to-year, the difference between the baseline and the budget is always the main-

---

[10]Since we are assuming that community college budgets and enrollments will move similarly to K–12, we can execute this test using only K–12 numbers.

tenance factor. A final footnote in the description of these tests is the role of maintenance factors.

Maintenance Factors

Maintenance factors serve to keep a running record of where K–12 education should be under Proposition 98 (the baseline) and where it is after the addition of the low-growth provisions included in Proposition 111 (the budget). In years when the General Fund grows faster than inflation, a portion of this shortfall (the maintenance factor) is restored to K–12 education until it gets back to baseline levels of funding. This restoration takes place in any year where the per-capita General Fund outgrows inflation (per-capita personal income) and a maintenance factor exists $(A2_t < N2_t)$. In these years, one-half of the difference in growth rates between the per-capita General Fund and inflation times the General Fund is required to be allocated to K–12 education in addition to the Test 1 or Test 2 amount. Equation (D.12) describes this relationship mathematically, where R_t is the amount to be restored to the budget in year t.

$$R_t = \max\left[\min\left\{ 0.5 \left(\left(\frac{H_t}{H_{t-1}}\right) - \left(\frac{J_t}{J_{t-1}}\right) \right) G_t, N2_t - A2_t \right\}, 0 \right] \text{(D.12)}$$

We have now covered all of the tests and their related pieces; the next section describes how they interact in a given year.

SELECTING THE CORRECT BUDGET AMOUNT

From the preceding part of the analysis, we have identified three amounts, one from each test—$A1_t$, $A2_t$, and $A3_t$. Which of these possibilities actually happens in a given year is governed by the following logic. The test that determines which equation to use compares growth in the General Fund per capita with growth in personal income per capita. If the General Fund growth is large by this test, then the budget equals the larger of amount $A1_t$ versus amount $A2_t$ plus the restoration R_t. If the General Fund growth is small by this test, then the budget equals the amount $A3_t$, represented in equations (D.13) through (D.15).

$$\text{If} \left(\frac{H_t}{H_{t-1}} \right) > \left(\frac{J_t}{J_{t-1}} \right) - 0.005 \qquad \text{(D.13)}$$

$$\text{Then } B_t = \max\left(A1_t, A2_t + R_t\right) \qquad \text{(D.14)}$$

$$\text{Else } B_t = A3_t \qquad \text{(D.15)}$$

One of the crucial aspects of California's K–12 finance structure is that it is dynamic—that is to say, each year is dependent on what happened in the prior year. This means that changes in any given year, such as those associated with the voucher initiative, can have effects on the baseline and budget numbers across all succeeding years. This is why it is necessary to develop a full dynamic simulation model, as we have done, to assess the prospects for K–12 education under different scenarios.

E. MODELING PROPOSITION 174: THE VOUCHER INITIATIVE

Modeling Proposition 174 has some interesting challenges, most of which are a function of the multitude of scenarios one is forced to consider. In this appendix, we review the basic model and components of the voucher initiative and then turn to the special cases and scenarios we considered in our analysis.

PROPOSITION 174 BASICS

There are several aspects of the voucher initiative that are common to all of the scenarios we reviewed. These commonalities include the cost of the scholarships and savings in each scenario. In order to facilitate our discussion here, we will use the following conventions.

i: An index measure, representing the number of years that year t is from the base year.

σ_τ: The proportion of students in year t who, without vouchers, would have attended public schools but choose instead, under vouchers, to attend private schools.

B_t: The Proposition 98 state and local commitment to education in year t. It equals the K–12 portion of the state General Fund and those local property taxes allocated for K–12 education. It does not necessarily equal the total commitment to public K–12 education, which is listed below as T_t. This is because certain provisions of the voucher initiative allow this amount to be offset by other items.

C_t: Total proceeds per pupil in public K–12 education in year t.

D: The eventual target proportion of students who, without vouchers, would have attended public schools but choose instead, under vouchers, to attend private schools.

E_t: Total K–12 enrollment in public schools in year t.

F_t: Total federal dollars going to public K–12 education in year t. Because the distribution and composition of the students shifting is unclear, we have assumed that these dollars are independent of the number of students in public schools and that all of the dollars remain in the public schools.

K_t: Total K–12 enrollment in private schools in year t.

L_t: Total lottery proceeds to public K–12 education in year t. We have assumed that these dollars are independent of the number of students in public schools. See Appendix C for a detailed discussion.

O_t: Total of other local proceeds to public K–12 education in year t. We assume that these, too, are independent of the number of students in public schools.

T_t: Total state spending on public K–12 education in year t.

U_t: Total state spending on all K–12 education in year t.

V_t: Total cost of scholarships redeemed in year t.

W_t: Total minimum amount of a scholarship in year t.[1]

X_t: The portion of local property taxes allocated to K–12 education in year t.

Z_t: Total amount of "savings" in year t, as defined in Proposition 174.

---

[1]Given the current fiscal crisis facing California, we have assumed that the state finances vouchers at the minimum level possible.

Note in these definitions that there are some important delineations that are slightly different from those in Appendix D. These differences will become clearer as we define and explain the model.

With this set of conventions, we can now define our voucher model. There are three definitions that remain constant across all of the scenarios—the calculation for the amount of the scholarship, the total scholarship costs, and the total savings as defined by Proposition 174. Subdivision (a) paragraph (1) of the initiative states that scholarships shall be at least one-half of the prior year's spending on public students, as we have listed in Equation (E.1).

$$W_t = \left(0.5\right) \times \frac{\left(T_{t-1} + X_{t-1} + F_{t-1} + L_{t-1} + O_{t-1}\right)}{E_{t-1}} \tag{E.1}$$

The total cost of vouchers is simply this number times the number of private students, as shown in Equation (E.2).

$$V_t = K_t \times W_t \tag{E.2}$$

The total amount of the savings, as defined in the initiative, is given by Equation (E.3) as the average per-pupil public cost times the number of private students, net the cost of the scholarships.

$$Z_t = \left[\frac{\left(T_t + X_t + F_t + L_t + O_t\right)}{E_t} \times K_t\right] - V_t \tag{E.3}$$

In addition, we are interested in analyzing the voucher initiative along two important dimensions—the effect of the initiative on total per-pupil resources available to public K–12 students and the total cost to the state of providing K–12 education to its residents.[2] The former measure is the sum of all the revenue streams in the public sector divided by the number of public students, as shown in Equation (E.4).

---

[2]The introduction to Chapter Four includes a further discussion of why these measures were chosen.

$$C_t = \frac{\left(T_t + X_t + F_t + L_t + O_t\right)}{E_t} \tag{E.4}$$

The other dimension of interest is the total cost to the state of providing K–12 education to its K–12 population, including public and private costs. This is given by Equation (E.5) in which total spending equals the public General Fund cost plus the private General Fund cost plus those local property taxes allocated to public K–12 education.

$$U_t = T_t + X_t + V_t \tag{E.5}$$

These equations apply universally across all of the scenarios we are presenting below.

MODELING THE SHIFT OF STUDENTS

Modeling the shift of students from public to private schools is quite straightforward. We have chosen to use a linear phase-in of the target shift level D over eight years, starting in the 1993–94 school year. The specified target level is converted to a yearly shift amount (σ_t) as given in Equation (E.6) for each year from 1993–94 to 2000–01, where i equals the number of years after 1992–93 (e.g., for 1993–94: i = 1, 1994–95: i = 2). In years after 2000–01, σ_t is set to D to reflect the fact that D percent of the students who would have attended public schools without vouchers are now attending private schools.

$$\sigma_t = i \times \frac{D}{8} \tag{E.6}$$

To arrive at the actual enrollment levels in year t, we start with the Department of Finance projections of the number of students in public and private schools over the next decade, calling them K^0 and E^0. Given a shift of σ_t in year t, each year's public and private enrollments are given by Equations (E.7) and (E.8), respectively.

$$E_t = E_t^0\left(1 - \sigma_t\right) \tag{E.7}$$

$$K_t = K_t^0 + \sigma_t E_t^0 \qquad \text{(E.8)}$$

The resulting quantity, E_t, is the value used in the Proposition 98 Test 2 and 3 calculations under vouchers.

MODELING THE STATE SPENDING POLICY CHOICES

Let us now turn to modeling each of the scenarios we have introduced in Chapter Three. They are "Minimum," "Full Budget," "Maintain State Effort," and "Hold Harmless." In addition, we will address each of them in the context of the "Double-Hit" or "No-Double-Hit" assumption. The general flow of analysis of each year is first to calculate the Proposition 98/111 amounts, deriving B_t, and then to analyze how Proposition 174 will affect the distribution of that pool of income.

Minimum

In the minimum-spending scenario, the state is spending the minimum amount required under the interpretation of Proposition 174 as it interacts with Propositions 98 and 111. The initial calculation is done by determining the Proposition 98 guarantee amount, B_t, using the methodologies described in Appendix D and the modified student populations shown above.

In the "Minimum" scenario, under the double-hit assumption, the total state minimum expenditure on public K–12 education in Tests 1, 2, and 3 is given in Equation (E.9) as the Proposition 98 guarantee less scholarships and savings. Equation (E.9) also applies to the Test 1 no-double-hit scenario.

$$T_t = B_t - X_t - V_t - Z_t \qquad \text{(E.9)}$$

Total state spending on K–12 is given by Equation (E.5) as the total quantities expended on public education. Similarly, total per-pupil public expenditures are given by Equation (E.4).

In Test 2 and 3 worlds, the form of T_t is shaped by whether there is a double hit or not. If there is no double hit, total state spending on public K–12 education is given by Equation (E.10), which is the state share of the Proposition 98 guarantee.

$$T_t = B_t - X_t \qquad \text{(E.10)}$$

Full Budget

In the "Full-Budget" scenario, the "savings" offset from the Proposition 98 guarantee are added back into K–12 spending. In the double-hit scenarios for Tests 1, 2, and 3, Equation (E.8) is modified as shown in Equation (E.11), in which the savings, V_t, are added back into total state spending on public education. It also applies in the Test 1, no-double-hit scenario.

$$T_t = B_t - X_t - V_t \qquad \text{(E.11)}$$

In the no-double-hit scenarios under Tests 2 and 3, there are no adjustments to Equation (E.9) as savings were never removed from the equations.

Maintain State Effort

The presumption in the "Maintain-State-Effort" scenario is that the state will maintain its total commitment to K–12 education as if vouchers had never occurred. The methodology in this system requires calculating the Proposition 98 guarantee under the initial public enrollment (E^0) estimates and then taking the total guarantee under this scenario (B^0) in a given year and dividing it out between the public and scholarship-redeeming schools. The formula for T_t in this scenario is given by Equation (E.12).

$$T_t = B_t^0 - V_t \qquad \text{(E.12)}$$

Note that the double-hit debate has no relevance in this scenario as the state chooses to finance K–12 education at a level higher than the minimum.

Hold Harmless

In the "Hold-Harmless" scenario, the state chooses to preserve the per-pupil resource levels in the public sector that would have been expected if vouchers had never happened. The public per-pupil expenditure, C_t, given in Equation (E.4) above is held constant through the provision of additional state funding. This is done by calculating the baseline per-pupil public expenditure (C^0) using K^0 for each year t and then using this to arrive at the value for T_t in this scenario, as given by Equation (E.13).

$$T_t = C_t^0 \times E_t \qquad \text{(E.13)}$$

Again, the double-hit debate has no relevance in this scenario as the state chooses to finance K–12 education at a level higher than the minimum.

F. TEXT OF PROPOSITION 174: THE PARENTAL CHOICE IN EDUCATION INITIATIVE

The following Section, the "Parental Choice in Education Amendment," is hereby added to Article IX of the California Constitution:

Section 17. Purpose. The people of California, desiring to improve the quality of education available to all children, adopt this Section to: (1) enable parents to determine which schools best meet their children's needs; (2) empower parents to send their children to such schools; (3) establish academic accountability based on national standards; (4) reduce bureaucracy so that more educational dollars reach the classroom; (5) provide greater opportunities for teachers; and (6) mobilize the private sector to help accommodate our burgeoning school-age population.

Therefore: All parents are hereby empowered to choose any school, public or private, for the education of their children, as provided in this Section.

(a) Empowerment of Parents; Granting of Scholarships. The State shall annually provide a scholarship to every resident school-age child. Scholarships may be redeemed by the child's parent at any scholarship-redeeming school.

    (1) The scholarship value for each child shall be at least fifty percent of the average amount of State and local government spending per public school student for education in kindergarten and grades one through twelve during the preceding fiscal year, calculated on a statewide basis, including every cost to the State, school districts, and county offices of education of maintaining kindergarten and elementary and sec-

87

ondary education, but excluding expenditures on scholarships granted pursuant to this Section and excluding any unfunded pension liability associated with the public school system.

(2) Scholarship value shall be equal for every child in any given grade. In case of student transfer, the scholarship shall be prorated. The Legislature may award supplemental funds for reasonable transportation needs for low-income children and special needs attributable to physical impairment or learning disability. Nothing in this Section shall prevent the use in any school of supplemental assistance from any source, public or private.

(3) If the scholarship amount exceeds the charges imposed by a scholarship-redeeming school for any year in which the student is in attendance, the surplus shall become a credit held in trust by the State for the student for later application toward charges at any scholarship-redeeming school or any institution of higher education in California, public or private, which meets the requirements imposed on scholarship-redeeming schools in Section 17(b)(1) and (3). Any surplus remaining on the student's twenty-sixth birthday shall revert to the state treasury.

(4) Scholarships provided hereunder are grants of aid to children through their parents and not to the schools in which the children are enrolled. Such scholarships shall not constitute taxable income. The parent shall be free to choose any scholarship-redeeming school, and such selection shall not constitute a decision or act of the State or any of its subdivisions. No other provision of this Constitution shall prevent the implementation of this Section.

(5) Children enrolled in private schools on October 1, 1991, shall receive scholarships, if otherwise eligible, beginning with the 1995–96 fiscal year. All other children shall receive scholarships beginning with the 1993–94 fiscal year.

(6) The State Board of Education may require each public school and each scholarship-redeeming school to choose and administer tests reflecting national standards for the purpose of measuring individual academic improvement. Such tests

shall be designed and scored by independent parties. Each school's composite results for each grade level shall be released to the public. Individual results shall be released only to the school and the child's parent.

(7) Governing boards of school districts shall establish a mechanism consistent with federal law to allocate enrollment capacity based primarily on parental choice. Any public school which chooses not to redeem scholarships shall, after district enrollment assignments based primarily on parental choice are complete, open its remaining enrollment capacity to children regardless of residence. For fiscal purposes, children shall be deemed residents of the school district in which they are enrolled.

(8) No child shall receive any scholarship under this Section or any credit under Section 17(a)(3) for any fiscal year in which the child enrolls in a non-scholarship-redeeming school, unless the Legislature provides otherwise.

(b) Empowerment of schools; Redemption of Scholarships. A private school may become a scholarship-redeeming school by filing with the State Board of Education a statement indicating satisfaction of the legal requirements which applied to private schools on October 1, 1991, and the requirements of this Section.

(1) No school which discriminates on the basis of race, ethnicity, color, or national origin may redeem scholarships.

(2) To the extent permitted by this Constitution and the Constitution of the United States, the State shall prevent from redeeming scholarships any school which advocates unlawful behavior; teaches hatred of any person or group on the basis of race, ethnicity, color, national origin, religion, or gender; or deliberately provides false or misleading information respecting the school.

(3) No school with fewer than 25 students may redeem scholarships, unless the Legislature provides otherwise.

(4) Private schools, regardless of size, shall be accorded maximum flexibility to educate their students and shall be free from unnecessary, burdensome, or onerous regulation. No regulation of private schools, scholarship-redeeming or not,

beyond that required by this Section and that which applied to private schools on October 1, 1991, shall be issued or enacted, unless approved by a three-fourths vote of the Legislature or, alternatively, as to any regulation pertaining to health, safety, or land use imposed by any county, city, district, or other subdivision of the State, a two-thirds vote of the governmental body issuing or enacting the regulation and a majority vote of qualified electors within the affected jurisdiction.   In any legal proceeding challenging such a regulation as inconsistent with this Section, the governmental body issuing or enacting it shall have the burden of establishing that the regulation: (A) is essential to assure the health, safety, or education of students, or, as to any land use regulation, that the governmental body has a compelling interest in issuing or enacting it; (B) does not unduly burden or impede private schools or the parents of students therein; and (C) will not harass, injure, or suppress private schools.

(5) Notwithstanding Section 17(b)(4), the Legislature may (A) enact civil and criminal penalties for schools and persons who engage in fraudulent conduct in connection with the solicitation of students or the redemption of scholarships, and (B) restrict or prohibit individuals convicted of (i) any felony, (ii) any offense involving lewd or lascivious conduct, or (iii) any offense involving molestation or other abuse of a child, from owning, contracting with, or being employed by any school, public or private.

(6) Any school, public or private, may establish a code of conduct and discipline and enforce it with sanctions, including dismissal. A student who is deriving no substantial academic benefit or is responsible for serious or habitual misconduct related to the school may be dismissed.

(7) After the parent designates the enrolling school, the State shall disburse the student's scholarship funds, excepting funds held in trust pursuant to Section 17(a)(3), in equal amounts monthly, directly to the school for credit to the parent's account. Monthly disbursals shall occur within 30 days of receipt of the school's statement of current enrollment.

(8) Expenditures for scholarships issued under this Section and savings resulting from the implementation of this Section shall count toward the minimum funding requirements for education established by Sections 8 and 8.5 of Article XVI. Students enrolled in scholarship-redeeming schools shall not be counted toward enrollment in public schools and community colleges for purposes of Sections 8 and 8.5 of Article XVI.

(c) Empowerment of Teachers; Conversion of Schools. Within one year after the people adopt this Section, the Legislature shall establish an expeditious process by which public schools may become independent scholarship-redeeming schools. Such schools shall be common schools under this Article, and Section 6 of this Article shall not limit their formation.

(1) Except as otherwise required by this Constitution and the Constitution of the United States, such schools shall operate under laws and regulations no more restrictive than those applicable to private schools under Section 17(b).

(2) Employees of such schools shall be permitted to continue and transfer their pension and health care programs on the same terms as other similarly situated participants employed by their school district so long as they remain in the employ of any such school.

(d) Definitions.

(1) "Charges" include tuition and fees for books, supplies, and other educational costs.

(2) A "child" is an individual eligible to attend kindergarten or grades one through twelve in the public school system.

(3) A "parent" is any person having legal or effective custody of a child.

(4) "Qualified electors" are persons registered to vote, whether or not they vote in any particular election. The alternative requirement in Section 17(b)(4) of approval by a majority vote of qualified electors within the affected jurisdiction shall be imposed only to the extent permitted by this Constitution and the Constitution of the United States.

(5) The Legislature may establish reasonable standards for determining the "residency" of children.

(6) "Savings resulting from the implementation of this Section" in each fiscal year shall be the total amount disbursed for scholarships during that fiscal year subtracted from the product of (A) the average enrollment in scholarship-redeeming schools during that fiscal year multiplied by (B) the average amount of State and local government spending per public school student for education in kindergarten and grades one through twelve, calculated on a statewide basis, during that fiscal year.

(7) A "scholarship-redeeming school" is any school, public or private, located within California, which meets the requirements of this Section. No school shall be compelled to become a scholarship-redeeming school. No school which meets the requirements of this Section shall be prevented from becoming a scholarship-redeeming school.

(8) "State and local government spending" in Section 17(a)(1) includes, but is not limited to, spending funded from all revenue sources, including the General Fund, federal funds, local property taxes, lottery funds, and local miscellaneous income such as developer fees, but excluding bond proceeds and charitable donations. Notwithstanding the inclusion of federal funds in the calculation of "State and local government spending," federal funds shall constitute no part of any scholarship provided under this Section.

(9) A "student" is a child attending school.

(e) Implementation. The Legislature shall implement this Section through legislation consistent with the purposes and provisions of this Section.

(f) Limitation of actions. Any action or proceeding contesting the validity of (1) this Section, (2) any provision of this Section, or (3) the adoption of this Section, shall be commenced within six months from the date of the election at which this Section is approved; otherwise this Section and all of its provisions shall be held valid, legal, and uncontestable. However, this limitation shall not of itself preclude an action or proceeding to challenge the application of this Section or any of its provisions to a particular person or circumstance.

(g) Severability. If any provision of this Section or the application thereof to any person or circumstance is held invalid, the remaining provisions or applications shall remain in force. To this end the provisions of this Section are severable.

G. SELECTED EXCERPTS FROM THE CALIFORNIA CONSTITUTION AND EDUCATION CODE

This appendix presents the actual text of sections of the California Constitution and Education Code cited in the other appendices.

CALIFORNIA CONSTITUTION ARTICLE XVI, SECTION 8

(a) From all state revenues there shall first be set apart the moneys to be applied by the state for support of the public school system and public institutions of higher education.

(b) Commencing with the 1990–91 fiscal year, the moneys to be applied by the state for support of school districts and community college districts shall not be less than the greater of the following amounts:

(1) The amount which, as a percentage of General Fund revenues which may be appropriated pursuant to Article XIIIB [the Gann limit], equals the percentage of General Fund revenues appropriated for school districts and community college districts, respectively, in fiscal year 1986–87.

(2) The amount required to ensure that the total allocations to school districts and community college districts from General Fund proceeds of taxes appropriated pursuant to Article XIIIB and allocated local proceeds of taxes shall not be less than the total amount from these sources in the prior fiscal year, excluding any revenues allocated pursuant to subdivision (a) of Section 8.5, adjusted for changes in enrollment and adjusted for the change in the cost of living pursuant to paragraph (1) of subdivision (e) of Section 8 of Article XIIIB.

This paragraph shall be operative only in a fiscal year in which the percentage growth in California per capita income is less than or equal to the percentage growth in per capita General Fund revenues plus one half of one percent.

(3) (A) The amount required to ensure that the total allocations to school districts and community college districts from General Fund proceeds of taxes appropriated pursuant to Article XIIIB and allocated local proceeds of taxes shall equal the total amount from these sources in the prior fiscal year, excluding any revenues allocated pursuant to subdivison (a) of Section 8.5, adjusted for changes in enrollment and adjusted for the change in per capita General Fund revenues.

(B) In addition, an amount equal to one-half of one percent times the prior year total allocations to school districts and community colleges from General Fund proceeds of taxes appropriated pursuant to Article XIIIB and allocated local proceeds of taxes, excluding any revenues allocated pursuant to subdivision (a) of Section 8.5, adjusted for enrollment.

(C) This paragraph (3) shall be operative only in a fiscal year in which the percentage growth in California per capita personal income in a fiscal year is greater than the percentage growth in per capita General Fund revenues plus one half of one percent.

(c) In any fiscal year, if the amount computed pursuant to paragraph (1) of subdivision (b) exceeds the amount computed pursuant to paragraph (2) of subdivision (b) by a difference that exceeds one and one-half percent of General Fund revenues, the amount in excess of one and one-half percent of General Fund revenues shall not be considered allocations to school districts and community colleges for purposes of computing the amount of state aid pursuant to paragraph (2) or (3) of subdivision (b) in the subsequent fiscal year.

(d) In any fiscal year in which the school districts and community college districts are allocated funding pursuant to paragraph (3) of subdivision (b) [Test 3A] or pursuant to subdivision (h) [suspension of Proposition 98], they shall be entitled to a maintenance factor, equal to the difference between (1) the amount of the General Fund moneys which would have been appropriated pursuant to subdivision (b) had subdivision (b) not been suspended, and (2) the amount of General Fund moneys actually appropriated to school districts and community college districts.

(e) The maintenance factor for school districts and community college districts determined pursuant to subdivision (d) shall be adjusted annually for changes in enrollment and adjusted for the change in the cost of living pursuant to paragraph (1) of subdivision (e) of Section 8 of Article XIIIB, until it has been allocated in full. The maintenance factor shall be allocated in a manner determined by the Legislature in each fiscal year in which the percentage growth in per capita General Fund revenues exceeds the percentage growth in California per capita personal income. The maintenance factor shall be reduced each year by the amount allocated by the legislature in that fiscal year. The minimum maintenance factor amount to be allocated in a fiscal year shall be equal to the product of General Fund revenues from proceeds of taxes and one-half of the difference between the percentage growth in per capita General Fund revenues from proceeds of taxes and in California per capita personal income, not to exceed the total dollar amount of the maintenance factor.

(f) For purposes of this section, changes in enrollment shall be measured by the percentage change in average daily attendance. However, in any fiscal year, there shall be no adjustment for decreases in enrollment between the prior fiscal year and the current fiscal year unless there have been decreases in enrollment between the second prior fiscal year and the prior fiscal year and between the third prior fiscal year and the second prior fiscal year.

(g) *There is no subdivision (g).*

(h) Subparagraph (B) of paragraph (3) of subdivision (b) may be suspended for one year only when made part of or included within any bill enacted pursuant to Section 12 of Article IV. All other provisions of subdivision (b) may be suspended for one year by enactment of an urgency statute pursuant to Section 8 of Article IV, provided that the urgency statute may not be made part of or included within any bill enacted pursuant to Section 12 of Article IV.

EDUCATION CODE SECTION 41203.5

(a) In any fiscal year in which the amount of the moneys that are required to be applied by the state for the support of school districts and community college districts is determined under paragraph (3) of subdivision (b) of Section 8 of Article XVI of the California Constitution, a supplemental appropriation shall be made from the General Fund for the support of those entities in that sum by which the amount determined under that paragraph is exceeded by the amount computed under subdivision (b) of this section.

(b) The amount of the General Fund revenues required to assure that the rate of growth in total allocations per unit of average daily attendance to school districts and community college districts from General Fund proceeds of taxes appropriated pursuant to Article XIIIB of the California Constitution, excluding any revenues allocated pursuant to subdivision (a) of Section 8.5 of Article XVI of the California Constitution, and allocated local proceeds of taxes is not less than the rate of growth in per capita appropriations for all other programs and services from General Fund proceeds of taxes appropriated pursuant to Article XIIIB of the California Constitution, excluding any revenues allocated pursuant to subdivision (a) of Section 8.5 of Article XVI of the California Constitution.

(c) In no event shall the total amount appropriated in any fiscal year pursuant to this section and paragraph (3) of subdivision (b) of Section 8 of Article XVI of the California Constitution exceed the amount which would have been computed pursuant to paragraph (2) of subdivision (b) of Section 8 of the California Constitution.

H. SENSITIVITY OF THE RESULTS TO THE DEMOGRAPHIC, ECONOMIC, AND INFLATIONARY ASSUMPTIONS

In order to perform this analysis, it is necessary to make many assumptions about the future prospects of the state's demographics, economics, and inflation rates. In this appendix, the sensitivity of our model to various ranges of inputs along these dimensions is analyzed. For comparative purposes, the high-shift (34 percent) scenario with a double-hit is displayed, although we have run sensitivity analyses for all of the scenarios under all of the sensitivity tests that follow. Only this one scenario is displayed in the interests of parsimony and because the effects under the other scenarios discussed in this report were directly comparable.

DEMOGRAPHIC ASSUMPTIONS

One of the key categories of assumptions in this model centers around the size of the state's future general and K–12 populations, both public and private. Accordingly, we ran the model using the low and high series for each of these populations described in Appendix A. Figure H.1 shows the policy space diagram reflecting the results of this sensitivity analysis.

As illustrated in Figure H.1, the demographic assumptions cause the entire policy spaces (including the baselines) to shift entirely up or down. The conclusion is that, while changes in the demographics of the model will affect the actual values of the results, they will not affect the overall relationships. Since our analysis centers on the relationships between the various scenarios and assumptions and not the actual results, our model is robust with respect to the demographic assumptions.

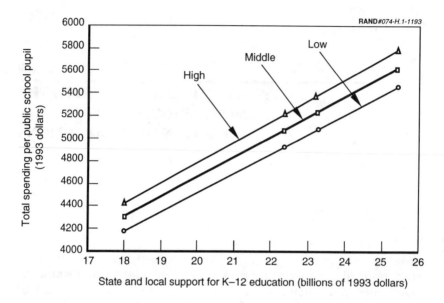

Figure H.1—Sensitivity of Results to Demographic Assumptions

ECONOMIC ASSUMPTIONS

The status of the state's General Fund and personal income plays a key role in the determination of the finances available to K–12 education as well. There is significant uncertainty about the state's economic prospects over the next couple of years, and even more about the longer-term prospects. For this reason, we have created wide bands of uncertainty about our underlying economic assumptions. The methodology for establishing these bands is given with the model in Appendix B.

In addition, property taxes play a key role in K–12 finance. Since they are a function of property values and tax rates within the state, their future levels are also uncertain. We developed a set of tolerance widths to assess the uncertainty associated with the future stream of these revenues. The details of this methodology are described in Appendix C.

In Figure H.2, which describes our economic sensitivity analysis, we used the high values for both the economic (General Fund revenues and personal income) and property tax assumptions.

As Figure H.2 shows, moving to the low or high economic and property tax assumptions shifts the entire policy space left (low assumptions) or right (high assumptions) along the same line as the middle scenario. We have separated them here stylistically to show the actual range of the alternative policy spaces. In actuality, they all fall on the same line. Since the shifts are proportional relative to the baselines (they shift too), the net effects on the overall policy space are also proportional and do not affect our conclusions.

The one effect of shifting the economic assumptions was to change the test deciding K–12 finances in 1995–96 from Test 1 to Test 2. As a result, the conspicuous initial downward spike in the "Minimum" and "Full Budget" in Figures 4.10 and 4.11 disappears. However,

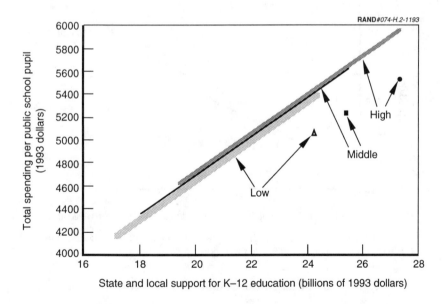

Figure H.2—Sensitivity of Results to Economic Assumptions

the downward jump in 1997–98 to 2000–01 in these figures remains. This was the only scenario in which varying the economic assumptions affected the relationships between the different series.

INFLATION ASSUMPTIONS

Finally, we have used an inflation factor of 3 percent throughout this analysis to be conservative. Figure H.3 presents the results in our example case using different inflation scenarios.

The shifts are all proportional and do not affect the relationships we discuss in our results, although they again affect the actual values. Given the robustness of our model under these various sensitivity analyses, we can move on to what these findings mean to the voters of the state.

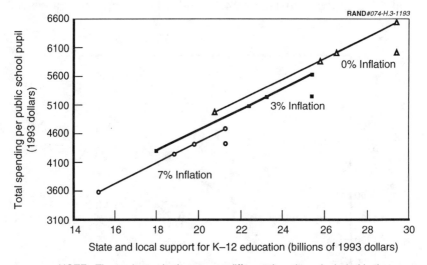

NOTE: The scales on both axes are different than those included in the other policy space diagrams in this report.

Figure H.3—Sensitivity of Results to Inflation Assumptions

I. DYNAMIC FISCAL CONSEQUENCES OF PROPOSITION 174 UNDER A NO-DOUBLE-HIT SCENARIO

The no-double-hit assumption affects all of the scenarios we will consider in this analysis. One aspect of the dynamics of the effects of Proposition 174 under the no-double-hit scenario is worthy of particular mention. This scenario arises when we go from a Test 2 to Test 1 world. Figure I.1 demonstrates this point.

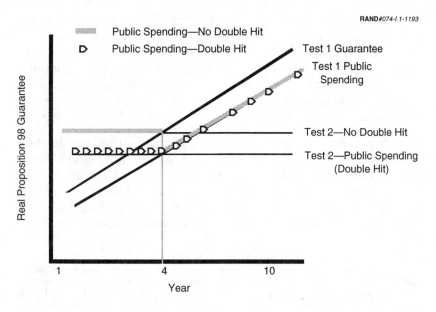

Figure I.1—Example of Voucher Finance Effects

In this diagram, which is intended only to demonstrate a potential effect of the "no-double-hit scenario," we have assumed that the shift from public to private schools has already occurred and that the number of both public and private students remains constant over time. The line labeled "Test 1 Guarantee" represents the Test 1 calculation based on General Fund revenues, and its upward slope represents an assumption that the real General Fund will grow over time. The line labeled "Test 2—No Double Hit" represents the Test 2 minimum Proposition 98 guarantee under a no-double-hit assumption, where public K-12 education receives the entire Proposition 98 guarantee and scholarships are funded from additional state funds. Since we assume there is no enrollment growth and the graph is shown in real terms, this is a flat line. The third line on the graph, "Test 1 Public Spending," represents the amount that is actually required to be spent on public education under vouchers in a Test 1 world.[1] The fourth line, labeled "Test 2—Public Spending (Double Hit)," represents the Test 2 minimum guarantee over time if there is a double hit. It represents the Test 2 guarantee net of scholarships and savings. Notice that it falls below the original scenario as the expenditures for vouchers and savings are counted toward spending.

In a double-hit scenario, the Proposition 98 minimum guarantee amount would be equal to the greater of "Test 1 Guarantee" or "Test 2—No Double Hit," resulting in a shift from Test 2 spending to Test 1 spending in year 4. Under the double hit, however, the expenditures on scholarships plus the savings would count toward these totals. For the public schools' purposes, therefore, actual spending would move along the lower lines, as shown by the small flags.

In contrast, the no-double-hit world counts savings and scholarships toward the Proposition 98 minimum only in Test 1. The selection of whether one is in a Test 1 or Test 2 world (selecting the greater of the two) occurs independent of this action. When there is a transition from a Test 2 year to a Test 1 year, a likely event under a high-shift scenario, there is a perturbation in the funding stream to the public

---

[1] Remember that Proposition 174 calls for the counting of the voucher expenditures and savings, as defined in the initiative, toward overall Proposition 98 minimum spending requirements. This has the effect of reducing the amount required to be spent on public students by the public per-pupil student cost times the number of private school students.

sector. Year 4 in Figure 3.1 demonstrates this effect, as the state goes from a Test 2 to a Test 1 world, as defined by the overall guarantee amounts. Because of the language in the initiative, the minimum guaranteed funds available to the public schools dip from the line labeled "Test 2—No Double Hit" down to "Test 1 Public Spending" in year 4, resulting in a sudden disruption to public school funding. A comparable upward shift occurs when shifting from a Test 2 to a Test 1 world.[2]

This problem is exacerbated by the use of prior-year revenues to determine the amount of the voucher in a given year. In the first year of a transition between a Test 2 and a Test 1 year, the scholarship is calculated based upon the prior year's public funding levels. However, public funding was much higher in the prior year than in the current year due to the effect described above. This means that not only does the public portion of the Proposition 98 guarantee offset by the amount of the scholarship, but it is offset by an amount that is much higher than the public schools are guaranteed in the current year.

Additionally, the size of the scholarships to scholarship-redeeming schools would be correspondingly reduced in the next year. Under this scenario and spending policy (unlikely but possible under the initiative), private schools would also be subject to massive shifts in their anticipated revenue streams. We have not discussed this issue in detail because it occurs in only one scenario under a narrow set of spending policies. It is important to note its possible occurrence, however, and to take actions in the implementation of the voucher initiative, if passed, to mitigate or avoid it.

_____

[2]Similar shifts would occur when shifting between Test 1 and Test 3 worlds. There is no such transitional effect when shifting between Test 2 and Test 3 worlds.